PRAGYANLOKAH

SCIENCE OF YOGA AND METAPHYSICS IN FOLK FESTIVALS OF KOSAL REGION

GOREKHNATH SAHU

Contents

Preface

The science of yoga so popular once upon a time, in the Aryan age, cannot be described in a plain and simple language. Yoga teaches us the methods of physical, mental, spiritual and social wellbeing. Yoga means, according to Jogeswar lord Srikrishna, "Karmasu Kausalam". It also means "Samatwam yogauchyate". To Maharshi Patanjali, it is 'Chittabrutti nirodhah'. The above three definitions of yoga have interrelation with one another and they are complimentary to one another. The first one means through yoga one can accomplish all works successfully or it is the best of all works. And the second one means to see all as equal and the third one means yoga is nothing, but sheer control of passions (Indriya). It is true that without control of passions no one can see all in an equal way nor can one achieve success in life.

The highest achievement in one's life is to merge with the infinite Paramatma: the Omnipotent, Omniscient and Omnipresent. This is called Mokshya. Yoga aims at this merger of the Atma with the Paramatma. Some believe this merger is possible only after death and some others like Maharshi Sri Aurobindo believe that the merger is possible even during the life time of a person. This is called the Jeevanmukti. This Jeevanmukti is possible only through 'Samadhi'. Sri Aurobindo has said that true spirituality starts only after Samadhi and before that everything is a preparation for true spirituality. He propounded the theory of ascent of the self and descent of the supramental. It is believed that Sri Aurobindo could bring about descent of the supramental himself during his life time.

Maharshi Patanjali is described by Swami Vivekananda as the greatest evolutionist on earth for discovering the theory and practice of Astanga Yoga; Yama, Niyama, Asana, Pranayama, Pratyahara, Dharana, Dhyana and Samadhi. They are not like eight steps or stages to be practised one after another, but to attain success they have to be practised simultaneously. This is called 'akramam'. Niyama aims at perfection of the individual, but Yama aims at perfection of the society, the nation or the humanity. Asana and Pranayama are meant to keep the human body and mind in good working order. Swami Vivekananda rightly complimented Maharshi Patanjali for the later gave the world a complete formula for a successful life and Salvation.

The last three Angas (limbs) Dharana, Dhyana and Samadhi together are known as "Samayam". The practice of which makes life sublime and opens the gateway to God, the eternal, the supramental, the Brahaman or the Paramatman!

In days of yore yoga was popular not only with the saints and seers, but also with the common people belonging to labour and peasant class. The more learned people in the science and art of yoga used to help their less fortunate brothers and sisters to achieve the goal of life in material as well as spiritual world. A wonderful tradition was established in this field which could be visualized in the folk festivals of Kosal region.

In all the folk festivals of Kosal region (Western Odisha) where-ever there is varua tattwa the principles of Astanga Yoga play their parts. One may wonder at this metaphysical discovery made by this author, but it is as true as broad daylight. To believe in such a spiritual phenomenon and to know the truth one has to undergo the subtle principles of Astanga Yoga of Maharshi Patanjali. It is not very difficult to conceive, but one has to show a little interest in it if he or she is a Sadhak or Sadhika or even curious about gaining secret knowledge of yoga.

Like any other spiritual knowledge and practices the science of yoga has undergone speedy degeneration. Yoga demands always the sacrifice of the self, but as ill luck would have it such folk festivals based on the foundation of yoga are taken for granted as festivals of animal sacrifice. Even in certain such festivals human sacrifice also takes place. Before independence human sacrifice was offered in the tribal folk festivals of the Kosal region. Though there is law against animal sacrifice ignorant people do not abide by it and take bestial pleasure in the sacrifice of innocent animals which cause degeneration of both economy and spirituality.

Now-a-days animal sacrifices are so rampant in the folk festivals of this region that one finds it difficult to attune these festivals to the intrinsic principles of yoga. The contents of this book will clarify all the doubts in the mind of the reader and take him or her to the realm of truth and find out to one's amazement the absurdity in such animal sacrifice which is unethical even irreligious on the part of the functionaries of such festivals. The time demands an immediate come back to its original spiritual status.

The purpose of writing this book is to unfold the truth about the folk festivals of the Kosal region which area is though economically poor, but spiritually extremely rich. This author has prepared an audio-visual documentary to establish this fact which is available, along with other publications of this author, in the Priambada Prakashani sales centre, Baishali Market Complex, Subarnapur.

CHAPTER ONE

WHAT MADE ME THE METAPHYSICAL DISCOVERY

I remember my childhood as early as I was three years old. I remember the behaviour of my parents, the other relations, other persons around me and my family. I have noticed more peculiarities in them rather than their normal human character. May be due to 'Prarabdha' or the previous birth I showed little interest in worldly life. I was a little different from all other children around me. The basic quality I noticed in me was a sense of detachment Later I came to know that it was the sense of non-attachment the cardinal principle of Srimat Bhagavat Geeta. As a result I left home in 1962 as a student of class X of M.R.High School, Sonepur with a motif to renounce the world and study in an ashram at Haridwar. I went to Raipur of Chhattisgarh and stayed in a dharmasala namely Satyanarayan Dharmasala near Raipur Railway station and waited eagerly for Triveni Bana Naga Baba of Sonepur a 'Siddha Sadhu' to come and join me for onward journey to Haridwar. I waited for him for long seven days, but he didn't like my idea of renunciation and instead waited for my return till all the money in my pocket was exhausted. In the mean time I came across a retired professor of Patna University, Bihar State, who knowing my intention asked me to go through Bhagabat Geeta which I had not read till then. I purchased a copy that night with translation in Hindi and read the same whole night. The professor at dawn knocked at my door and asked me what I understood. In reply I told him that for renunciation we need not leave home. Even while staying at home we can practise renunciation. He agreed and advised me to go back home and suggested you can come when you retire from your family life. I obeyed him and returned home, but my heart and soul remained in some unknown ashram of Haridwar and I long to be a monk even today.

All through my life I have been trying to be a good man by doing good to others and by doing something good for the society. I have been involved in many public movements and have also suffered imprisonment in movement like that of Sonepur Trust Fund. There has been gun firing by the police in the anti Manivadra Dam movement where Atal Bihari Mohapatra a student of law then, now an advocate, was seriously injured and I along with some activists were luckily saved from the gunshot. In the meantime I got married and became the father of four children. The world around me couldn't content me and I was anxious to go to Munger, the Bihar School of Yoga to learn the lessons of yoga from proficient teachers. It was towards the last part of eighties when the curiosity to know and practise yoga was very insatiable in me. At that juncture appeared in my life a yoga teacher earlier known to me as our Team Manager of Sambalpur University Football team playing tournament at Patana of Bihar and later he became a relation in a family way. He is yogacharya prof.

Jayadev Dansana who has a good knowledge of Astanga yoga of Maharshi Patanjali and its application. He started a yogalaya namely Sri Gopaljee Yogalaya in the premises of Sri Gopaljee Temple of Sonepur where I joined as a member and later became its Executive President. Every day during his stay Sri Dansana used to spend a good deal of time in yoga class in deliberation (manan) about the principles of yoga. It is very interesting to note subjects of yoga as they spring out of his mind by way of accumulation of knowledge through vast reading of books on yoga written by noted authors of national and international repute.

During his discourse prof. Dansana used to highlight on the seven symptoms of 'Samadhi' the Spandan (termor), Ghurni (zyration), Udvab (levitation), Anand (elation), Nidra (drouze), Murchha (swooning) and Jagruti (awakening). All such symptoms appeared to me like a dream and suddenly I found them all in the 'barua' of Bali Yatra of Sonepur. During my childhood my father used to carry me on his shoulders like other parents with their children and help me witness the famous Bali Yatra of Sonepur. At that time a large number of people used to see such spectacular spiritual phenomena which has degenerated with the ravages of time due to lack of faith, and knowledge and patronage of such spiritual folk festival. After long thirty years I again witnessed the Bali Yatra and to my amazement my intuition proved true and I danced in utter joy. My joy knew no bounds and I invited some of my friends including Prof. Dansana to witness and realize the truth about my discovery. Some of them were half convinced, other were not convinced and to my surprise I found Prof. Dansana not very much convinced. In fact my strong intuition got the ultimate grace of God which guided me to make my discovery full-proof on scientific lines. I wrote several articles on the same subject matter captioned "Sonepur bali jatrare astanga yogara pratifalana: eka abiskar." I contributed the same article to the daily Samaj as I was its acting journalist. The article was published in bold letters with many photographs of bali yatra. The article was appreciated by the intelligentsia of the state which attracted the attention of persons like Sabyasachi Mohapatra the noted film maker. Sri Mohapatra happens to be a close friend of my family, also he was my classmate in law college at Sambalpur who wanted to make a documentary on my research. He immediately summoned his photographer brother Prakash from Mumbai and successfully made the documentary with the title 'Samadhi'. However, Sri Mohapatra used to ask me a question as to how the ignorant and uneducated 'baruas' not having any knowledge and practice of yoga could enter into the state of trance or lower Samadhi. Here again my intuition worked hard and my obvious reply to him was the effect of the 'Sabdabrahma' the drum-beat with 'Sohala varani'. I was in search of some written document which will satisfy myself and persons like Sabyasachi Mohapatra. God is so kind who gave to my hand document after document to put-forth my point of view in a very scientific and strong manner. First of all I came across a book namely 'Patanjali Yogasutra' in English written by Swami Pravabananda Saraswati and Christofer Iserwood where I got the time frame for concentration, meditation, lower Samadhi (trance) and Nirbikalpa Samadhi.

Even after that my instinct of search after truth was not satisfied and I strove again and again to reach the foundation of such a colossal structure which was built by our forefathers as the best gift to mankind.

I had contributed an article captioned "Sonepur bali yatra : yoga, nrutya, geeta o loka Sanskrtira eka ananya santaka" which was pblished in the Loka Mahotsava Souvenir 1999 of Sambalpur at page 04-07 of chapter Loka Sanskruti. The article revealed the intrinsic yogic principles applied and manifested in the famous bali yatra of Sonepur. The article could not satisfy the searching mind of Sabyasachi Mohapatra. I was also in a dilemma for about two years. I failed to find a suitable answer as to how the 'baruas' could enter into the state of trance. It is rightly said if one searches deeply with a perfect sense of devotion he will find God on his way. Again God's Grace was showered on me and I was prompted to go through an article written by prof. D.G.Bishi on "Shakta Pramoda Badya Tattwa" published in the same souvenir at page 01-04 in chapter 'Loka badya and loka nrutya'. To my utter surprise the article was on the "Shohala varani badya" the popular drum-beat in bali yatra of Sonepur which I have been hearing with heart throbling enchantment from my childhood sitting on the shoulder of my father to witness clearly the divine movement of 'barua'. The shohala varani badya is part and parcel of 'Shakta Pramoda badya Tattwa which later I discovered from a scholar that the same was scribed as palm leaf manuscript and the inventor was one tantric Adivasi Santha named Sonar Sang of village Rohillaka the modern Rohela near Binitapur (modern Binika) in Subarnapur district. The shakta pramoda badya Tattwa or Shohala varani drum beat is exclusively meant to guide the mental force of a barua or varua whose body and mind are filled with the daivishakti or divine energy. The science of such badya tattwa has been clearly discussed in detail in another chapter of this book. Thank God!

My search is complete with three important books: Mind, its Mystery and control by Swami Shivananda Saraswati as regards the symptom of trance, the lower Samadhi, second book- 'The Patanjali Yoga Sutra' written by Swami Pravananda and Christofer Iserwood where the time frame of lower Samadhi is mentioned and the third is the article written by Prof. Dr.D.G.Bishi, originally scribed in palm leaf manuscript, by an Adivasi saint named Sonar Sang of village Rohela near Binika of Subarnapur district, where the science of sound is mentioned that guides and helps the barua in divine dance from the beginning to the end means from varani to chhadani. In the long run Swami Vivekananda has answered the question how the ignorant and the uneducated go to the state of Lower Samadhi by saying that 'a fool goes to sound sleep returns a fool and a fool goes to Samadhi returns a sage'. However, many other questions struck my mind which were answered through very valuable books like Sri Vijgyan Vairaba Tantra, 'the Ascent' by Swami Satyasangananda Saraswati, 'Mind and Super Mind' by Sri N.C.Panda, 'Serpent of Fire' by Darrel Irving. For this work I am compelled to think about God's Grace and for that reason I fold my hands to that Omniscient in heartful gratefulness. I only remember the story of the poem 'the Ballad of Father Gilligan' who knelt down and prayed,

'He who is wrapped in purple robes
Hath planets in his care
Had pity on the least of things
Asleep upon a chair'.

CHAPTER TWO

THE HISTORICAL BACKGROUND OF KOSAL REGION AND ITS FOLK FESTIVALS

"Geographical condition including the nature of the land and the climate in Kosal Region have contributed immensely towards the birth and growth of festivals. A society which is forced to spend more time on procurement of goods or things for satisfying the minimum necessities of life has less time for festivals, whereas a society which has plenty of leisure is likely to have more of festivals.

The society in Kosal Region like the society in other part of India, is very old and has a history dating back to several centuries. People must have had plenty of leisure in the past as a result of which we have a very rich depository of festivals in all parts of Kosal Region.

Whatever might have been the fate of the rulers of this region, the people of Kosal lived a very rich life. The undulating landscape dotted with colourful mountains having varieties of flora and fauna and rich valleys. The innumerable rivers, both small and great, and the temperate life-giving and invigorating climate-all gave the people of this region a befitting stage for enacting the drama of life in a variety of ways. Unconcerned about who the rulers were and what they did, the non-tribals and the tribals alike lived a life of toil, intermixed with dance, drama, music and song. Consequently, the people of this region inherited a rich cultural heritage in different forms of festivals. Each part of the landscape of Kosal Region is distinct from the landscape of any other part in the region. There is no monotony of the landscape here as in the plains. All the seasons are full of different varieties of flowers and scents. And all this is reflected in the bewildering variety of its festivals.

The rulers of the erstwhile princely states of Kosal Region were great devotees of Devi Durga. Consequently, every ruler constructed a temple dedicated to Devi Durga or one of her several incarnations within the premises of his palace. And every year in the month of Aswina a yatra or a ritual was organized to celebrate the occasion. These rituals continue to be performed even to-day though the princely states and the rulers are no longer there. The chhatar jatra of Bhawanipatna in Kalahandi district, the Bali jatra at Subarnapur in Subarnapur district, the Patakhanda jatra of Jarasingha in Bolangir district and the Khandabasa jatra of Nuapada in Nuapada district, the Kantkuanri jatra of Bonai in Sundargarh district, the Kuanri jatra of Debgarh in Debgarh district are well known festivals associated with this worship. During the celebrations elaborate rituals of different kinds based on local customs are performed in different places.

An important feature of the ritual at different places of Kosal Region is offering of animal sacrifice to appease the

Goddess. This practice of offering the animal sacrifice to Goddess is obviously based on a superstitious belief the origin of which is difficult to trace. But the native rulers encouraged such practices to frighten their gullible subjects and keep them under their control. In recent years, however, voices are being raised against this practice and in some places it has been discontinued.

In the words of Sri Rama Chandra Mallik a noted historian the author of 'Kosal Itihas' "the students are the backbone of the nation. They build the future of the society. Therefore, the students should read and know about the glorious history of the past of their forefathers. They should be acquainted with various aspects of their past lives. Then only they can rebuild the present with utmost care and diligence. To gather knowledge about the past should be the first and foremost duty of the students of any nation and they can pass on to their successors such knowledge for the betterment of the society. Ram Chandra Mallik as a historian has appealed to the students and the general public to read and gather knowledge about the rich and glorious history of Kosal Region, the contribution of the rulers and their subjects. He has mentioned about the history of greater Kosal namely "Bruhat Kosal Itihas" in two thousand one hundred and fifty pages written both in English and Odiya that has been preserved in the Odisha State Archives at Bhubaneswar.

Kosal as a geographical boundary exists since the Ramayana age. The name is associated with Raghuveer Sri Ram Chandra the epic hero of the Ramayana who happened to be the eldest son of king Dasaratha of Ayodhya and his Maharani Kausalya. Maharani Kausalya is mentioned as the princess of the Kosal kingdom. Sri Ram Chandra, one of the incarnations of lord Vishnu, was also addressed as Kosaladhipati as he adorned the throne of Kosal Empire. Later his younger son Kusha was given the charge of rule of the South Kosal. However Kausalya, Kosaladhipati, Kusha they are all linked with Kosal which did not lose its identity historically. The formation of the state of Odisha comprised the three separate zones namely Utkal, Kalinga and Kosal. The Kosal region, from Ramayana time experienced and established a great cultural tradition. It had relationship with the Ram Rajya of Kosaladhipati, Sri Ram, the benevolent king of Ayodhya. The social condition during Ram Rajya has been described vividly in the scripture of Ramayana when people lived happily and peacefully. There was no want of any kind. The subjects were contented with what they had. They had firm faith in their king and God. They got instant justice at their doors. For the sarcastic comment of a washer woman on Maharani Sita, Sri Ram Chandra drove her out of the palace at a time when she was in the family way. Thus was the character of a ruler who was better known as 'maryadapurusha' who in order to keep his father's words preferred fourteen years banishment to occupation of royal throne. He was the embodiment of humility (namrata), a yogi par excellence, a philosopher king endowed with all the good qualities of God! He was not only godly, but God incarnation in true sense of the term. He had great influence over his subjects. What is a character? Character is simply a habit long continued. Festivals are part and parcel of a culture. The rural folk are basically associated with the forest, flora and fauna, with nature. They are nearer to the creation of God, hence they are nearer to God, the Creator!

Here we come across the impact of the Ramayana civilization on the rural folk of Kosal region. The urbanization, the growth of township has adversely affected the custom and tradition of the rural folk of the Kosal region, but such impact has not been successful in wiping out their faith in God. There age-old custom and tradition, their folk culture, their folk festivals etc, above all their way of life. They are more attached to their mother tongue, their motherland and their mother culture. In the process the people of Kosal region have been able to protect and preserve their mother-tongue and mother-culture against all odds.

The folk life of Kosal predominantly belongs to the schedule tribe, schedule caste and other backward class who by nature are honest and simple. They have least craze for material gain. They seldom tell a lie and do not like to cheat others. They are always ready to give and fight shy to receive. They lead a life of contentment and thus attain peace and happiness. Forgive and forget is the motto of their life. They are never revengeful in their attitude. They follow the following principles in life:

"dharyam jasya pita, kshyama cha janani,
shantischiram gehini, satyam sunurayam,
daya cha bhagini, bhrata manh sanjamah,
sajya bhumi talam, dishopi basanam,
gyanamrutam bhojanam,
ete jasya kutumbino badasakhe kasmat bhayam yoginah!
(Geeta)

Patience, forgiveness, peace, truth, kindness, self control, simple living, thirst for knowledge are the basic qualities of a yogi.

All these heavenly qualities make their mind clean.

"Mana nirmala jara dehi,
Uddhaba Ganga jala sehi".
(Bhagabat)

The human mind which is as clear as a mirror is the right place for concentration and meditation as pratyahara is easy in such a mind and that becomes the right abode of God!

The rural folk of Kosal region carry on the spiritual and cultural tradition of the Ramayana age. They have imbibed the spiritual tradition from their ideal ruler Sri Ram Chandra who was a yogi par excellence. The cultural tradition of Kosal region is essentially the spiritual tradition which encompasses the total life force of the people of this region. Their food, cloth and shelter, their dance, drama, music and song, their love life and their worldly life all surround this spiritual tradition and the spiritual tradition is based on the intrinsic principle of yoga. The last three angas of Astanga yoga dharana, dhyana and Samadhi, are known as samayama.

What a great spiritual tradition has been established by the rural folk of the Kosal region in the form of the 'Barua Tattwa' that has been fitted into almost all the folk festivals of Kosal region. The Kosal region comprises the districts of Sundargarh, Jharsuguda, Debgarh, Sambalpur, Bargarh, Subarnapur, Bolangir, Nuapada, Kalahandi and the Sub-division of Athmallik of Angul district. Ofcourse, other districts of divided Koraput such as Malkangiri, Rayagada, Koraput and that of Navarangpur also follow almost the same spiritual tradition in their cultural life alongwith the Kosali language and culture. The advasis like Soura tribe live even today a life in trance out of which they derive all answers to their questions and all solutions to their problems. This sounds quite ridiculous, but it is quite true. We have to believe that there is a life beyond our knowledge, in the words of Albert Einstein. The rural life in Kosal region is more akin to such mystery and thus more akin to the supernatural, unknown to their urban counterpart.

This provides the backdrop of such folk festivals in Kosal region which go on unabated since time immemorial, may be from the time of Sri Ram or Parshuram the Aryan hero who anhihilated twentyone times the Khyatrias and made this world nikhyatriya and perhaps during that period the tribal folk adopted the principle of 'Samayama' of Astanga Yoga and put them in practice in their folk festivals and derived out of them immense peace and pleasure. This practice of 'Samayam' (dharana, dhyana and Samadhi) is the only way out to enter into the realm of the mysterious world of the Creator! Thus our fore-fathers were able to cultivate this supernatural aspect of life. Surprisingly enough they were extremely successful people in attainment of spiritual goal.

As contentment is the prelude to peace and peace is prelude to happiness, so is happiness a prelude to nityananda or paramananda, the true nature of God! Here the negative philosophy of Buddhism fails. The world is not only full of sorrow, but also it is full of 'ananda' which is the positive aspect of Sanatan Dharma. Hindu Santhas like Kumaril Bhatt sacrificed their lives in propagating against such negative attitude of Buddism and in favour of positive attitude of Hinduism. It is true that negative attitude breeds negative results and positive attitude breeds positive results. For that reason the 'three monkey guru' of Mahatma Gandhi adopted from Buddist scriptures should also be discarded as they approach in a negative way to see no evil, hear no evil and say no evil as psychology forbids such negative approach and therefore they should be replaced by 'neo three monkey guru' who profess positive attitude by indicating 'see good, hear good and say good'. The three positive attitudes will prompt a person to do good ultimately and thus by doing good one becomes a good man. By becoming a good man he becomes a divine being in accordance with the will of God the father of all beings. (The concept of Neo three Monkey Guru is evolved by this author who propagates such theory by making terracotta, wooden and metallic monkeys).

This is the real secret of the spiritual tradition of Kosal region. The Barua Tattwa aims at divinization of the body (matter) and transformation of the mind. It also aims at changing the society by making more and more prophets who will help in changing the Kaliyuga into Satya Yuga. Only strict adherences to yoga can bring about such a change. The 'baruas' are from some selected class of the community. They lead a very pious life in austerity. They are treated as demi-gods. Their life style, behavior, food and drink habit, their purple attair, long hair make them distinct from other common men in the society. They always remain engrossed with the thought of particular god or goddess which they call their 'ista' deva or devi. This is called the ekatma bhava with the presiding deity. This helps them to attain the state of concentration and meditation.

The most important aspect in almost all the folk festivals of Kosal region is the role of the sohala varani drum beat which has been utilized as the part of Shakta Pramoda Vadya Tattwa. Sound system or sabda brahma has direct relation with the subtle function of the human mind and with the system of nerves and tissues. The inventor had the perfect knowledge of such effect on the body and mind of human beings. It is the sound that activates and controls the actions and reactions of the 'barua', the person in trance. The other sebayats including the priest only check and balance the 'barua' in a state of trance. The priest, no doubt, applies yantra, mantra and tantra for proper guidance of the 'barua'. The chargharias keep on guard over the 'barua' and the musicians play on music with utmost sincerity. It takes more time to bring a nuakuanri (initiated for the first time) to a state of trance as concentration is more difficult for such a newcomer, but it is not always true as it is a matter of the mind and a newly initiated person may have better ability for concentration which has been proved. Even a person at a distance enters into a state of trance being influenced by the sound of the drum beat.

Folk Festivals: Past and Present

This spiritual tradition of the highest order enlisted the royal patronage during the ex-state rule. The kings, princes along with their relations used to participate actively in such folk festivals. They had distributed permanent maufi landed properties in the name of the sebayats with royati status. They had also sufficient land and other properties in the name of the deities for their regular seva puja. The public participated in such spiritual functions with a great sense of respect and reverence. Everywhere there was large gathering and people, both men and women with their children, used to enjoy the celebrations to the fullest contentment of their heart and soul. They used to offer huge amount of 'Samidha' and pure cow ghee for the purpose of homa or jangya. This used to keep the environment clean, free from bacteria and helped good shower of rain which ultimately helped the production of bumper crop. Thus the whole spiritual act aimed at wellbeing of all, means the mental satisfaction which establishes mental peace and happiness. The wellbeing of the subjects was the aim and objective of the royal patronage of such functions. The sebayats of various caste and creed were not only respected, but also their demands were given due importance by the royal administration. So, the general public also had a great sense of respect for such sebayats. For example the priest (purohit) performing Bali Yatra at Sonepur was given maufi land and as a mark of respect he was invited to sit on the throne of Maharaja of Sonepur for one day which was scheduled on the day of 'dasahara' every year. There is a popular saying among the people "ekdinia purta raja ding dong kari bajla baja". The Baruas for Sonepur Bali Yatra hailed from village named 'Sakama' who enjoyed maufi royati land given by the royal administration of Sonepur ex-state. Now-a-days the festivals have been organized mostly by the public with least participation and patronage of the state administration. It is a half-hearted effort on the part of both the general public and the administrative authorities who do not understand the meaning and usefulness of such festivals.

No doubt other parts of the world might have been applying such scientific yogic principles in their own way and they might be calling the 'barua' in different names, but it is true that Kosal region stands first among them in the matter of long duration of time, grandeur in celebration, involvement of large sections of the society, establishing the permanent nature of the functions, huge area of operation etc.

The effect of such spiritual phenomena:

The effect of such spiritual phenomena is to bring about a happy social order in the region. Here the famous saying of swami Vivekananda, has to be viewed who said "spiritual development is the only development". The scientific sage is hundred percent true as there cannot be all-round development without spiritual development. The spiritual development not only helps personal development but also helps the social development. The spiritual development is defined in the 'astanga yoga' of Maharshi Patanjali: yama, niyama, asana, pranayama, pratyahara, dharana, dhyana and Samadhi. Yama means ahimsa, satya, astheya, brahmacharya and aparigraha. In English they are non-violence, truth, non-stealing, celibacy and non-receiving. Niyama means: soucha, santosha, tapa, swadhyaya and Iswara pranidhana which means in English-cleanliness, contentment, penace, self study and God realization. The other four limbs (angas) of astanga yoga are purely mental. Pratyahara demands the mental act to drive away all other thoughs except one to be concentrated. Dharana is to concentrate the mind on one subject matter and dhyana is to continue that concentration for a particular period of time (time frame discussed in a separate chapter). Samadhi happens automatically when dhyana continues for a particular period of time. Dhyana (meditation) can also be acomphished without dharana on any subject matter. It is told 'dhyanam nirbishayam manah'. Meditation is possible when the mind is devoid of any subject matter. There are 112 kinds of 'dharana' described in the book "Vigyana Vairaba Tantra". The Ascent, written by Satyasangananda Saraswati. The sum total effect of such spiritual phenomena is to derive the unknown and unseen from the mouth of the 'Varua' attaining godhood. The other effect is to get the divine blessings from the barua in Samadhi. It is not only mere spiritual faith or belief, but such faith is established under scientific yogic principles.

The degeneration of faith and the need for its revival

It is also a fact that there has been a degeneration in the faith cherished by the people as regards the spiritual aspect of the folk festivals of Kosal region. The reason of such degeneration is due to lack of knowledge on the part of the general public about the scientific principles what we call yoga. The development of the physical science has caused great impact on the spiritual science and thus has affected the human sentiment in respect of existence of God. In-fact there has been a speedy degeneration of faith in God which has adversely affected the faith in the daivi shakti (divine spirit) of the 'barua'. The lack of faith in barua tattwa has affected the sincere spiritual performance of the 'barua' in folk festivals of Kosal region. Despite the disinterestedness on all fronts the 'spirit' in the function has not died down completely. The light is burning and we have to put only a little more oil for its continuance and sustenance. One day will come when that light will show the spiritual path to the whole world again.

The spiritual tradition has to be revived at all costs. It is a necessity to keep the society going on the spiritual path. The tradition has to be kept up as it is the best spiritual tradition which has no parallel in the world. It has stood the test of time. It has sanction of the saints and seers of the days of yore who have sacrificed their lives on experiment to prove such spiritual tradition as the best of all. The general people of Kosal region are fortunate enough to explore and accept such a function for their spiritual life which is responsible for their social emancipation. The folk festivals of Kosal region have made the spiritual life of the people rich and has made their social lives still richer.

The question remains how the folk festivals of Kosal region will be revived. It is not a question of revival of the dead, it is a question of revival of the living for better health and strength. It will be sufficient to express in one word that it should be provided with patronage: both administrative and public. The public and administrative patronage are complementary to each other. Both should come forward to protect, preserve and augment such rich spiritual tradition by way of celebrating the folk festivals in the Kosal region which will naturally attract the attention of the people of the world. If yoga can become so popular why the cream of yoga will fall behind? I am astonished how and why people of this region miss such a good point in life? I feel they should put utmost stress on their spiritual life and maintain the grand tradition of their folk festivals. At this juncture the print as well as the electronic media should come forward to highlight the extraordinary spiritual tradition of the folk festivals of Kosal region which the viewers are eager to witness at least that part of the concentration, meditation and trance that happen to 'barua' in such folk festivals. That can be done by way of public projection and telecast in different channels of electronic media. The subject matter should be brought to the curriculum of the study in the school and college level. The students should be educated in their mother culture through their mother tongue.

CHAPTER THREE

PATANJALI YOGASUTRA MATERIALISED IN THE VARUA TATTWA

Patanjali yogasutra is like a mathematical formula by practice of which the spiritual height is attained. There is of course different gradation of spiritual excellence. The deeper one practises the higher one goes to attain this excellence in the realm of spirituality which finally helps in meeting the individual self with the universal or the divine self.

According to Patanjali yogasutra 'desha bandhaschittasya dharana' which means dharana or concentration is nothing but to centre round the mind with a spiritual thought or consciousness.

"Tatra pratyayeikatanata dhyananh' means unabated flow of similar thought or consciousness already established in the mind. 'Nadebarlhamatra nirvasam swarupa sunyamiba samadhih" means the unfoldment of the real truth of such subject matter (already held in dhyana) through dhyana or meditation. 'Trayamekatra samayamah' means through dharana, dhyana and Samadhi together the real truth of a subject matter is known and those three angas (limbs) together known as samayama.

'Tatjayat pragyanlokah' means by samayama the pragyanlokah (super intelligence or wisdom) is manifested.

'Sarbartha taikagratayoh kshyayadayoh, chittasya Samadhi parinamah' means when all types of mental fluctuations (chitta vikhepa) are driven out of the mind and the mind is concentrated on one point then the mind enters into the state of Samadhi. When the mind enters into the state of Samadhi then seven symptoms manifest in the body and mind of the same person. The seven symptoms are spandan (tremor), ghurni (gyration), udvav (levitation), ananda (elation), nidra (drowse) and jagruti (awakening).

It is a matter of great surprise that in folk festivals of the Kosal region the Baruas or varuas, deheris or dehelias are taken from the state of concentration and meditation to the state of trance (lower Samadhi) by utilizing the principles of yogasutra of astanga yoga of Maharshi Patanjali. The Kosal region is described by the UNDP as the most backward area economically, but it is very rich spiritually. Unless one sees such festivals with full knowledge of yogasutra of Patanjali one cannot conceive the spiritual excellence of such festivals which have degenerated into festivals of animal sacrifice and thus put the people in a state of shame. On account of the animal sacrifice in such folk festivals the people of Kosal region are termed as uncivilized, barbarians, uncultured and backward. In fact the folk festivals are the real hidden treasure of spirituality based on practical and scientific principles of yoga. Let the whole world see and know about it. This will, no doubt, revive the lost glory of the people of Kosal region.

In some of the folk festivals of Kosal region the varua (deheri, dehelia etc.) foretells the past, present and the future. It was the common belief that the varua tells the truth. This common belief now has degenerated to a great extent, but even today there are people who have full faith in the power of the varua whose knowledge is illumined in the state of Samadhi.

According to Patanjali "Parinama trayasyasamyamadati tanagatagyamnanr" which means by making samayama on the three kinds of changes, one obtains knowledge of past and the future.

This is believed as part of the occult power. This has been described by Patanjali in his Yogasutra how various occult powers and the methods by which they are acquired. All authorities like Ramakrishna Paramahansa, Lord Buddha, Jesus Christ including Patanjali regard occult powers as the greatest stumbling blocks in the path to spirituality and truth.

However, the occult power satisfies the instinct of man to know the unknown. This natural instinct though psychological, prompts for the ultimate material gains. The sincere spiritual aspirant can have very little concern with such matters. In the west, these powers are seldom exhibited, and are therefore, the object of a good deal of scepticism. 'The western man has preferred to concentrate on the production of mechanical rather than psychological powers: and so, instead of telepathy we have the telephone, instead of levitation we have the helicopter, and instead of clairvoyance we have television. Teleporting and telelife are yet to be invented. But Patanjali prescribed the method how one can be invisible. According to him if one makes samayama on the form of one's body, obstructing its perceptibility and separating its power of manifestation from the eyes of the beholder, then one's body becomes invisible. When the bonds of the mind caused by karma have been loosened, the yogi can enter into the body of another by knowledge of the operation of its nerve currents. 'The yogi, says Vivekananda, can enter a dead body and make it get up and move, even while he himself is working in another body, or he can enter a living body and hold that man's mind and organs in check, and for the time being act through the body of that man". The story of Shankara, Mundan Mishra and his wife Pravavati confirms the truth about this saying. By controlling the nerve current that govern the lungs and upper part of the body, the yogi can walk on water and swamps or on thorns and fire or similar objects, and he can die at will. By making samayama on the gross and subtle forms of the elements one gains the power of becoming as tiny as an atom. We may regret the materialism that is expressed by such a choice, but perhaps, it is the lesser of the two evils. So let us stop hankering after the psychic-powers and turn back to the true path towards spiritual growth, remembering Patannjali's warning. "They are powers in the worldly state, but they are obstacles to Samadhi".

It is a fact that the materialistic attitude to life has to a great extent, damaged the mental, psychological and spiritual life of man. The saints and seers of our motherland had striven very hard and dedicated their whole life in research and discovery of such fantastic phenomena to reach spiritual height of success which no other countrymen could ever perceive, but alas! At present we are shocked and surprised to see such unprecedented degeneration of spiritual feeling and growth among men which is disastrous to peaceful human living. The world is on the crossroads of destruction due to this materialism which has given birth to a demon called 'terrorism'. Swami Vevekanand told only the spiritual development can save the world from destruction and deluge. He also said that 'they only live who live for others'. So long man is selfish and goes on fighting among one another for selfish ends there is no stop to self-destruction and annihilation and the moment man sheds off selfish desire and thinks for the welfare of other beings then in no time Heaven will descend down on Earth and mankind will enjoy heavenly peace and happiness.

Without Samadhi there is no beginning of spirituality. Without spirituality there cannot be realization of the self. There cannot be the unfoldment of the truth by virtue of pure consciousness. "Antah karanare jatahoithiba Iswara darshanara gotie bindu utsaha, swargara lakhye mandira darshanara madhurjya tharu besi". A drop of desire to see God in one's ownself (antahkarana) is better than the sweetness of seeing a lakh of temples in the domain of Heaven. The desire to see God in one's ownself is accomplished only through Samadhi. Therefore, yoga aims at Samadhi which happens through practice of concentration (dharana) and dhyana (meditation). It is through concentration we see the difference between a man and an animal as we see the difference between a man and a man. It is concentration again which is responsible for the success of a man in any field of life. Obviously concentration is the most important part of yoga. It is therefore, rightly told by Jogeswar Krishna "Yoga karmasu kausalam". It is also rightly said by Patanjali that 'Chhittabrutti nirodhah yogah'. Without chittabrutti nirodha one cannot attain success in life. To accomplish everything in life it is imperative to control the sense organs and master over them. Perfection of the body includes beauty, grace, strength and the hardness of a thunderbolt. By making samayama on the discrimination between the sattwa guna and the Atman, one gains the power of omnipotence and omniscience. Perfection is attained when the mind becomes as pure as the Atman itself. It is, therefore, told by Rishi Jangyabalka that 'Atman Hrut Pratishtam' means atman's resting shrine is the heart. In Upanishad it is told that the atman is nothing but the still and un-hovering mind which in meditation moves from the brain and finally settles down at heart. This subtle truth can only be experienced and realized by a man in meditation. It is only through meditation one unites himself with the infinity, the real nature of God.

It is through meditation the varuas of the folk festivals of Kosal region enter into the state of trance (Samadhi) and unite themselves with the eternity and see the truth, the God. It is further told that 'Brahmabid Brahmeiva Bhabati' one who knows Brahma becomes Brahma himself. In folk festivals, therefore, the varua attains the qualities of gods and goddesses and thus worshipped by the people in absolute faith. They are treated in the society as uncommon among the common men. They are considered the moving gods and goddesses on Earth. They are revered by people for having a divine spiritual personality.

These folk festivals are celebrated in Kosal region as a great established spiritual tradition. This spiritual tradition had its link from the time of lord Parshuram who is believed to be immortal and still living. The tradition is still alive, may be with little forgetfulness and degeneration of spiritual knowledge and practice. This degeneration may be attributed to the cause of ignorance on the part of the elite people, the intellectuals, the administrative authorities who have become more and more materialistic and less and less spiritual in their outlook. Contrary was the practice and faith among their royal counterparts in the olden days.

The modern man believes that the materialistic attitude is the scientific attitude and separates science from spirituality, but indeed spirituality is nothing but the science of sciences, which the whole mankind should believe and know. Therefore, the true scientific attitude is the spiritual attitude to life which is the mother of all scientific inventions.

Dharana on Shabdhabrahman- The basic principles adopted in folk festivals.

'Annahate paatrakarne' bhagnashabde saniddrute;
Shabdabrahmani nishnaatah param
brahmaadhigachehhati'

This means one who is adept in listening to the unstruck sound in anahata, which is uninterrupted like a rushing river, attains the supreme state of Brahma by mastery of shabdabrahman, the form of Brahman as sound. In tantra we learn that there are two types of sound; audible (vaikhari) and inaudible (upansu) sounds. Nada yoga is a system of dharana which attunes the awareness to these subtle sound frequencies which are heard internally at the point of anahata chakra and which are unstruck in nature. There are ten such sounds; kini, kinkini, tantri, venu, kantha, veri, sankha (conch), mrudanga, tala, vajra. Nada or sound is the first evolutes of consciousness. In tantra the first word is the mantra AUM. The unstruck sound produced in the anahata is known as para nada but the sound struck by something with an object is 'vaikhari' and there can be dharana on such sound and with samayama on such sound one can attain the state of Samadhi which is being practised in the folk festivals of Kosal region.

The eight limbs of yoga are: the various forms of abstention from evil doing (yama), the various observances (niyama, posture (asana), control of the prana (pranayama), withdrawal of the mind from sense objects (pratyahara), concentration (dharana), meditation (dhyana) and absorption in the Atman (Samadhi).

Yama is abstention from harming others (ahimsa) from falsehood (satya) from theft (astheya) from incontinence (brahmacharya) and from greed (aparigraha).

The Niyama (observances are purity (soucha), contentment (santosha), mortification (tapa), study (swadhyaya) and devotion (iswarapranidhana) to God.

When a man becomes steadfast in his abstention from harming others (ahimsa) then all living creatures will cease to feel enmity in his presence.

When a man becomes steadfast in his abstention from falsehood (satya) he gets the power of obtaining for himself and others the fruits of good deeds, without having to perform the deeds themselves.

When a man becomes steadfast in his abstention from theft (astheya) all wealth comes to him. When a man becomes steadfast in his abstention from incontinence (brahmacharya) he acquires spiritual energy.

When a man becomes steadfast in his abstention from greed (aparigraha) he gains knowledge of his past, present and future existences.

As the result of the purity (soucha), there arises indifferences towards the body and disgust for physical intercourse with others.

As the result of contentment (santosha), one gains supreme happiness.

As the result of mortification (tapa) impurities are removed. Then special powers come to the body and the sense organs.

As a result of study (swadhyaya) one obtains the vision of that aspect of God which one has chosen to worship.

As the result of devotion to God (Iswarapranidhana) one achieves Samadhi.

Posture (asana) is to be seated in a position which is firm but relaxed. 'Sthiram sukham asanam'. Posture becomes firm and relaxed through control of the natural tenderness of the body and through meditation on the infinite.

Thereafter, one is no longer troubled by the dualities of sense experience.

After mastering posture, one must practice control of the prana (pranayama) by stopping the motions of inhalation and exhalation.

The breath may be stopped externally, or internally, or checked in midmotion, and regulated according to place, time and a fixed number of moments so that the stoppage is either protracted or brief.

The fourth kind of pranayama is the stoppage of the breath which is caused by concentration upon external or internal objects.

As the result of this, the covering of the inner light is removed.

The mind gains the power of concentration (dharana).

When the mind is withdrawn from the sense objects, the sense organs also withdrawn themselves from their respective objects and thus are said to imitate the mind. This is known as pratyahara which is successfully accomplished by the varuas in folk festivals of Kosal region.

Thence arises complete mastery over the senses.

Concentration (dharana) is holding the mind within a centre of spiritual consciousness in the body, or fixing it on some divine form, either within the body or outside it. The varuas in this connection concentrate over the God or Goddess of the respective places as the divine form and meditate on the same till the schedule time.

Meditation (dhyana) is an unbroken flow of thought towards the object of concentration. When in meditation the true nature of the object shines forth, not distorted by the mind of the perceiver, that is absorption (Samadhi).

When these three concentration, meditation and absorption are brought to bear upon one subject, they are called samayama.

Through the mastery of samayama comes the light of knowledge. This is purely a mental phenomena. This principle of samayama is practiced and mastered by the varuas in the folk festivals of Kosal region. They practice and perform the lower Samadhi which means the mind of the varua continues unabated in the state of meditation for twenty eight minutes and forty eight seconds.

When the vision of the lower Samadhi is suppressed by an act of conscious control, so that there are no longer any thoughts or visions in the mind, that is the achievement of control of the thought waves of the mind.

When the suppression of thought waves becomes continuous, the mind' is calm. When all mental distractions disappear and the mind becomes one pointed, it enters into the state of Samadhi.

The mind becomes one pointed when similar thought waves arise in succession without any gaps between them.

In this state, it passes beyond the three kinds of changes which take place in subtle or gross matter, and in the organs; change of form, change of time and change of condition. But the mind, in the state of Samadhi, is beyond all three kinds of changes.

The succession of these changes is the cause of manifold evolution.

By making samayama on the three kinds of changes, one obtains knowledge of past and the future.

The varuas of folk festivals of Kosal region do perform this kind of samayama and gain knowledge to predict the past and the future. Concentration may also be attained through devotion to Iswara (God). According to Patanjali Iswara is a special kind of Being, untouched by ignorance and the products of ignorance, not subject to karmas or samskaras or the result of action.

As a result of devotion to God, one achieves Samadhi. The varuas of the Kosal region are basically devotees of Gods and Goddesses. They adore in reverence the deities and worship them, pray them and chant their names (japam) time and again in devotion (bhakti). The varuas are also known as bhaktias means devotees. They are believed to be nearer such divine energy. They remain engrossed day and night in the thought of their God or Goddess and become one (ekatma) in union with them. For that matter the varuas before the beginning of meditation are kept in closed doors with the deity inside the temple which helps the varua in pratyahara (neti, neti) and concentration on the object of his devotion. In the state of Samadhi (trance) the experience and the object of experience become one and the same. Here the famous saying of Vedas; Aham Brahmasmi, Soham, Ayamatmabrahmah and Tatwamasi come true. In this state the barrier between the body (matter) and spirit (soul) is broken. The varua becomes himself the incarnation of such god or goddess held in concentration and meditation. In that state the Atman-the experience-is pure consciousness. It manifests as the light of knowledge. This is a very difficult task to understand by the ignorant but very easy to understand and perceive by the knowledgeable. In the state of awakening the varua becomes the source of all spiritual wisdom which is inside ourselves; that the kingdom of Heaven is within us where the citadel of the Lord is enshrined. This state of realization of the true spiritual aspirant is achieved through faith, energy, recollectedness, absorption (Samadhi) and illumination. This is absolutely true to the ardent devotees, the varuas of folk festivals of Kosal region.

CHAPTER FOUR

THE SCIENCE OF SHAKTA PRAMODA BADYA TATTWA OR SHOHALA VARANI BAJA

The shohala varani badya or the sixteen beats of drum are popularly used in the folk festivals of Kosal region. The Harijans or the Gandas by caste beat such drum known as dhola. A drum beater is assisted by other musicians who play mahuri, nishan, tasa, gini, ghanti etc. In the folk festivals of this region the drum beater is the hero among the musicians. The festivals are mostly meant to arouse the Kundalini of the varua or barua. The drum beat produces such 'sabda brahma' which naturally helps the Varua to tread on the path of dharana (concentration), dhyana (meditation) and finally Samadhi (the trance or ecstasy). The folk festivals of this region are observed with pomp and ceremony, basically, as spiritual functions where the varua is used as manifestation of Gods and Goddesses who dance to the tune of the beats of drum.

There are sixteen steps of the physical and mental stages of the varua when he or she undergoes such physical and mental transformation.

The sixteen types of drum-beats are named varani, ranjani, manjani, sammohani, sakti akarsani, anuprabesika, uddatadharini, prachanda, sirsabastiti, bilasa, anuranjani, shaktyabesha, abirvaba, chakramanjari, vimala and shantikara.

The first one of the sixteen beats known as 'varani' helps the varua, who sits or sleeps in a yogic asana, in creation of tremor (spandan) in all the limbs of the varua. This sound is produced specially on the combined basis of sadaja, gandhara and dhaibata dhwani as propounded by the specialists of music mentioned in the palm leaf manuscripts of the ancient time. The effort of varani badya (sound) makes the varua introvert and his senses become antarmukhi.

The second beat is known as 'ranjani' by which the tremor created by varani is spread through the length and breadth of the whole nervous system of the varua. With this beat of drum the tip of hair of the varua also start trembling.

The third beat is recognized as 'manjani' which establishes the previous sound and creates tremor in the dhwani (sound)chakras of the body of the varua. The echo of such sound is produced in each tissue of the body. These dhwani or sound chakras are discovered by the tribal music specialists in the past who had given importance to them for spiritual emancipation.

The fourth beat is 'sammohani' which takes the varua to the final state of pratyahara and makes his or her mind free from all other thoughts of the outside world. By this sound the varua enters into the stage of 'daibivilas'.

The fifth beat of sohala varani badya is 'shaktiakarshani' which means this sound attracts the yogic power of such God or Goddess on whom the varua had concentrated his or her mind in dharana. By this beat of drum the spiritual energy of such God or Goddess is invited with humble submission. Therefore, this beat is also locally known as abahana or welcome sound. With this beat of sound the varua starts hopping or dancing in tune of the beat of drum and sound of the music. At this juncture various miraculous actions and reactions manifest in the body of the varua which sometimes baffle the witnesses.

The sixth drum beat is 'anuprabeshika'. This sound is based on the raga Malashree which creates terrific blast of spandan (tremor) in the tissue chakra of the varua. In this state the varua loses his selfconsciousness completely and does not remember anything of the outer world. Now the varua starts dancing swinging his limbs in various pose and posture. This is called 'angakhela' in local language.

The seventh beat is called 'uddatadharini'. By this beat of drum the effect of anuprabesika is further extended and spread with a bang in all parts of the tissues (koshas) of all the limbs with the daibisakti or godly energy. In this stage the varua manifests very strange physical, vocal and mental symptoms. With this beat of drum the varua crosses the limit of his or her natural strength and exhibits angry moods and swift dances. The movement of the limbs of the varua is free and find completeness in this beat of drum for which this state is described as angkhela or play of the limbs.

The eighth beat of sholavarani badya (sound) is known as 'prachanda' in consonance with the deep intensity of the sound which similarly makes the varua attain one ugra (ferocious) rupa means very angry appearance. In this state the varua runs or jumps in great force, produces terrific sound or even seen kicking the musicians. With this beat the sahasrara chakra of the varua is vibrated. Before this beat there occurs vibration in other chakras such as Muladhara, Swadhistana, Manipura, Anahata, Bisuddhi, Ajna, Bindu etc.

The ninth beat is 'rasabastiti' locally known as 'sikhabandha' or 'chulabandha'. After 'sikhabandha' the varua is calmed down and his angry mood is vanished. The sound humbles his temper.

The tenth beat is 'vilasa'. This beat helps for the spread of the godly energy already created throughout the body and mind of the varua. Thus the spiritual attainment equally distributed among the tissues (kosha) of the varua in prashanta bhava(blissful state). In Kosali language this is called 'avisek' or rijhen'. In this state the varua attains the spiritual excellence and remains in a mood to bless the people without any discrimination. In this state the varua experiences laughter or cry. At this stage the 'sahasrara chakra' of the varua is fully illumined or awakened.

The eleventh beat is called 'anuranjani'. At this moment the body of the varua is sanctified with the daibibhava or the perception of the divine. He or she accepts the whole universe as the manifestation of the godly power. This beat, therefore, is also called 'rasabesh' which means the spread of divine juice. In this state the varua attains the true appearance of the God / Goddess and exhibits signs as a peaceful and blissful divine being.

The twelfth beat is named 'shaktyabesh'. At this stage the varua is tired of dancing. In order to prolong the divine power in the body of a person such power is kept controlled in the chula or sikha of the same person. It is said by the specialists in tantra that such divine power can be kept alive for only fourteen praharas means forty two hours. After that schedule time the stored divine power becomes gradually weaker and weaker. At this stage the divine power can be brought back in the body of the varua by such beat of drum known as chakar ulta or debtachadha means rejuvenation of the divine power or return of the divine power.

The thirteenth stage of the Shaktapramoda Badya Tattwa is known as 'abirbhaba' or known as 'uva' in the local language. In this stage the varua being totally pacified attains motherly qualities. In case the god or goddess shows sign of anger than the priest calms down the varua with the 'prasantashankari' mantra. This is what happens in the 'Baliyatra' of Sonepur when the varua demands, at times, sacrifice of man or animal. At this time the musicians are asked to produce soft sound to calm down the angry mood of the Varua.

The fourteenth stage is 'chakramanjari' which in the Kosali language is called 'chakarkeli' or chakarmara. In this beat the sound system is organized in the open kalachakra dhwani. At this stage the varua experiences gyration or ghurni. The varua's head or body gyrates clockwise or anticlockwise. At this stage the varua goes on changing his mood from stiffness to softness or sometimes follows the middle path and shows signs of steadiness. During this period the priest prays and seeks blessings for the devotees.

The fifteenth beat of drum is 'Vimala' which indicates the awakening of divine power in varua. It also indicates the gradual lusterless-ness of the varua. The signs of farewell of the divine power is thus imminent. At this stage the varua with motherly motives gives proper advice and blessings to the shakta devotees. Then the devotees shout joy joykar in praise of the god or goddess. This beat is known as 'urghen' in Kosali language.

The last beat of Shakta Pramoda Badya Tattwa is 'shantikara'. The God or Goddess is allowed to rest in peace at this stage. The sound is that of visarjan. The priest chants the mantra of visarjan at this time. The varua then falls flat and lies on the floor near the jodakhamba or under the chhatra or umbrella. In the local language this beat is known as chhaden.

AWAKENING IN BARUA

To elucidate the object of Raja Yoga Swami Vivekananda has stated "imagination properly employed is our greatest friend. It goes beyond reason and is the only light that takes us everywhere".

"The more powerful is the imagination, the more quickly the result be attained and Kundalini awakened. To raise the Kundalini is the complete object of "Raja Yoga"

Swamijee's version of "Raja Yoga is applicable to the folk festivals of Koshal region where the object of such festivals is to awaken the Kundalini in the Varuas of such festivals.

The tantras depict twelve chakras positioned along the spine. Seven are considered major and five are minor. The existence of the chakras is not seen through the ordinary physical eye, but they are described in greater detail by the saints and seers of the ancient age who could by deeper sadhana were able to see and perceive such existence and decipher their actions and reactions in a human body. They had, undoubtedly, supernatural knowledge about the physical, ethnic, astral, mental or casual bodies. The chakras have been described as nerve centres which govern the various organs as turning wheels.

It is said that the chakras serve as centres for the manifestation of various human emotions such as love, fear, anger and joy. It is further stated that what we experience in our lives depends to a certain degree upon the chakras to which we are attuned, for each chakra is energized by certain emotional, mental, physical and spiritual attributes. Those who are in touch with the lower chakras are more inclined to gratification of physical senses. Those who are capable to touch the higher chakras are inclined to intellectual and spiritual attainments. Accordingly, all people are in touch with the chakras and their vocational capacities are directly influenced by the chakras to which they are most directly connected. Thus chakras are viewed as energy centres and also are adjudged as gateways to other worlds, to other dimensions, the paranormal or the supernatural.

In tantra chakras are depicted as lotuses and as domains inhabited by Gods and Goddesses. It is important to note that the four elements-earth, water, fire, air and basic sounds, smells and sights are associated with the chakras. The five physical senses are also associated with the chakras. There are twelve chakras according to the text of tantricism. They are : mooladhara, swadhisthana, manipura, anahata, vishuddhi, ajna, lalana, nasikagra, manas, soma, bindu and sahasrara.

"Aamoolat kiranaabhaasaam sookshmaat sookshmataraatmikaam: Chintayetaam dvishalkaante shaamyanleem Bhairavodayah".

Fusion of prana and apana gives rise to the awakening and ascent of Kundalini through sushumna nadi. Paradevi manifests as kundalini shakti and entering the physical body, takes her seat at mooladhara chakra.

A psysic centre, or chakra is a vortex of energy, where many nadis converge and then redistribute this energy to different parts of the body. There are seventytwo thousand nadis in the physical body of a man. The word nadis means 'flow' or 'channel': it does not mean nerve. The nerves are the gross counterpart of the nadis which carry electrical impulses from the brain to the different parts of the body. The nadis carry subtle energy in the form of consciousness, or chittashakti and pranashakti. The nadis are invisible to the bare eyes, but can be perceived in the form of light by the inner eye. It is the power of pure awareness that assumes the form of a nadi.

The redistribution of energy to different parts of the body in a Varua can be described in the state of trance where the paradevi manifests as kundalini shakti. This is possible at the arousal of the mooladhara chakra of the Varua in the folk festivals of the Kosal region.

Dwadashanta means at the end of twelve and here refers to the sahasrara chakra at the top of the head, which is the seat of shiva as believed in tantricism the pure untainted consciousness. It also refers to the twelve chakras. Or psychic energy centres, through which the awakened energy passes, gradually becoming more and more subtle until it merges into sahasrara, which is the abode of the most subtle self situated at the end of these twelve chakras as described before. They constitute the pranic body and form the psychic passage of sushumna: with mooladhara at the base and sahasrara at the top. Pranashakti, which is sleeping at mooladhara chakra in the form of a coiled serpent, is known as kundalini. When the Kundalini ascends through sushumna, it opens these twelve chakras, one by one. In this way the experience of consciousness and energy becomes more and more subtle, and the feeling of peace and tranquillity arise. Same is the condition and feeling of the Varuas who fail to describe their inner experience in any expressive manner.

Just as a seed carries the inherent power to sprout and grow into a giant tree, a mantra has the inherent power to explode gross matter and transform it into energy. The bija mantras are like the missiles which travel at lightning speed, carrying the gross physical awareness to subtle and transcendental states. The 12 chakras and their corresponding bija mantras are as follows: mooladhara-lam, swadhistana-vam, manipura-ram, anahata-yam, visuddhi and lalana – ham and nasikagra-so. The bija mantra for all the higher chakras such as ajna, manas, soma, bindu and sahasrara is Aum.

The technique used to pierce these twelve centres requires a proper understanding of these mantras in relation to Varua roopa and nada or colour, form and sound. Each bija mantra is as potent as the chakra it represents. Dharana should be practiced on the respective bijas in their various aspects of colour, form and sound to open the chakras. In this way each chakra can be opened, one by one and the desired experience attained. As the kundalini ascends, the range of experience changes from gross to subtle. For example, the experience of colour will give way to sound or light, which are subtler forms of the same experience. All the mantras originate from word "akshara" means "indestructible", or that which never alters or dies. Aksharas are made up of dhwani or sounds of varying frequencies. This has relation with the shakta pramoda vadya tattwa described earlier. The sound frequencies guide the inner actions and reactions in the body and mind of a Varua. In order to explode the energy within the mantra, the dhwani has to be separated from the akshara.

There are fiftyone aksharas, which correspond to fiftyone energy centres in the physical body. These energy centres are connected to the different centres in the brain. Different aksharas constitute the different bija mantras, and with repetition they progressively influence the kundalini energy as it pierces through the twelve chakras, one by one and finally the shakti (kundalini) merge with Shiva (Sahasrara) and both become united as pure supreme consciousness.

The mind is the seat of awakening. The mind springs out of the brain matter in the body. The modern scientific research says that only 7% of the human mind is active in a common man. In the case of Newton and Adision their mind functioned up to 8% to 9%. In the case of Albert Einstein his mind functioned up to 11% and in the case of Shakuntala Devi, the human computer, her mind functioned up to 20% for which reason she could defeat a computer in competition. Swami Vivekananda had a very great functional mind who could remember many books by comma and full-stop even after reading the books once for all. He attributed this mental power to his strict observance of celibacy or 'Brahmacharya'. The mankind has not yet encountered a better mind than those mentioned above, but truly speaking the rest of mental faculty is still unknown to our scientists. Of course sincere research is going on in this field. However, the human mind and its capacity remains an enigma, for all the time, to human beings themselves, but from the scriptures we learn that the yoga rishis had better knowledge and practice in this field. They were "Trikalangya" who had knowledge of the past, present and the future. This mental power is possible only by yoga sadhana. It is again said that in the state of Nirbikalpa Samadhi, such knowledge is possible.

The human search is always from the known to the unknown. The modern scientists are now searching after the God particle (Ishwara kanika). This God paticle is nothing, but the soul or Atma. Astabakra muni, in the Raja-sava of Rajarshi Janaka clarified that the universe is the manifestation of the soul. The world before him believed that the soul is the manifestation of the universe. Astabakra muni just reversed the idea of creation, soul and the Omnipotent Paramatma. In Upanishad even the shape and size of the soul or Atma is mentioned whose shape and size is said to be the ten thousandth part of the tip of a hair. It is that God particle out of which the universe is created in a short span of time and it is that God particle which the scientists are in search after and which they claim to have found.

However, it is believed and scientifically found by Yoga Sadhakas that there are 12 chakras in the body of human beings which start from the Muladhara and end in the Sahasrara. By practice of asana, pranayama, dharana and dhyana the chakras are stimulated one after another. With the stimulation of the sahasrara chakra which is placed in the brain, the brain functions are accelerated and thereby its physical, mental and spiritual capacity is increased manifold. Hence unknown is known to the person concerned. He thus forecasts the past, present and future, may be in alien language not known to the person present nearby.

Thus the natural instinct to know the unknown is satisfied. Further by awakening of the Chakras the Sadhak enters into the blissful state of the mind which is compared with pleasant experience of coitus known as ecstasy, but discarded by the philosopher king Indrabhuti in his famous book 'Jyanasiddhi'. This is a wonderful experience which can be attained only by Sadhana of yoga. It is only through yoga one can achieve eternal peace and happiness in life. Who does not like to enjoy eternal peace and happiness and that is why the awakening of the chakras is necessary.

WHETHER A FOOL CAN GO INTO SAMADHI?

According to Swami Vivekananda 'a fool goes to sound sleep, returns a fool and a fool goes to Samadhi returns a sage'. This statement is by someone who is adjudged as the scientific sage of the world. Vivekananda does not accept anything without verifying the truth about it. He even verified the power of tantra and mantra, with a sadhu who could produce something out of nothing. It is evident from the saying of the seer that to enter into Samadhi or trance no formal education or wisdom or intelligence is required. According to him a fool can also enter into the state of Samadhi. When a fool goes to sound sleep he returns to sense again as a fool without any change in his attitude of spiritual life, but when a fool enters into the state of Samadhi he undergoes such spiritual experiences that he returns as a sage with the knowledge of true spirituality.

The statement of Swami Vivekananda is true to the spiritual life of the Varuas of the folk festivals of the Kosal region. In fact after entering into the state of trance (Samadhi) the Varuas lead a pious life and behave like sages. The common people in the society treat them as uncommon people and adore them like demigods and goddesses. The Varuas command utmost respect and reverence from other people and are considered as superhuman beings.

The Varuas of different folk festivals of Kosal region in their personal and family life adhere to the strict principles of Yama and Niyama of Astanga Yoga. They hail mainly from the peasant and labour class and asana and pranayama are very natural to their life style and in the folk festivals they only sit or sleep in the posture of yogic Asanas and for Dharana, Dhyana and Samadhi (Samayama) the Sohalavarani (sixteen beats of drum) badya does the miracle in taking the Varua from concentration to meditation and finally to the state of Samadhi.

Some people may think that the principles of Astanga Yoga are very difficult to understand and practise and beyond the grasp of the Varuas who belong to the lower strata of the society, but an introspection into their life will reveal the truth that every human being, who is a little spiritual, a little conscious, has some basic knowledge and practice of yoga. By nature every human being comes to this world with an objective of performing yoga seeking the final purusartha called mokshya (liberation). Ignorance about purusartha and yoga makes human beings beastilike. It makes them take many births to come to the path of yoga and mokshya.

However, it is seen from the day-to day life of the Varuas that they not only have the knowledge and practice of spirituality, but also their family members cherish such idea of concentration, meditation and trance. When interviewed they express their knowledge and belief in their own language in clear-cut terms. All the days the Varuas are associated with the festivals, they abstain from physical relationship with their spouse and lead a life of austerity; eating less and that too pure sattwik food, sleep on the mat on the floor, wear purple robes, keep the hair uncut, do not use oil or soap, do not take to alcohol or any kind of intoxication, remain calm and quiet, secluded from humdrums of life, concentrate on the desired deity and thus pass through a pious life. Although these days the Varuas prepare themselves spiritually and psychologically for that final moment of trance, the Samadhi, for some psychological and spiritual effect the Varua is treated with some bibhuti (ash) or sand or soil that is placed on his naval. The whole process is more mental and physical. The common viewer sees and enjoys the physical aspect of the glorious spiritual act. Such viewer witnesses the formal worship by the priest, the drum beat of the dholias, the dancing of the Varua, the killing of animals and birds, the music of other musicians, the action and reaction of other sebayats like chargharias, chhatrias etc. but the viewer with the knowledge of the Astanga Yoga with special knowledge of samayam (Dharana, Dhyana and Samadhi) will derive utmost pleasure out of such spiritual functions.

THE VALUE OF TRADITIONAL FOLK FESTIVALS:

What are the real values of such folk festivals? Why they are observed as a matter of tradition? What are its effect? How they are different from other spiritual functions? A lot of such questions arise in the mind of the readers which need to be answered for clarification.

There are different steps in the ladder of spiritual practice and God realization called Iswara Pranidhana according to astanga yoga. It may be different stages of realization. We may take the example of Swami Vivekananda who in his early age wanted to see God eye to eye, face to face. Even though Ram Krishna Paramahansa showed him Maa Kali face to face and eye to eye Vivekandnda did not stop there and in the later life he said. "Service to man is service to God". After this also he did not stop and in the last part of his life he said. "My boys play football, play on, there is divinity in football". This means "ehi stambhare dele mana, ehi stambare Bhagavana". In this saying we are reminded of the episode of Hiranyakashipu, Bhakta Prahallad and Nrusingha Avatara who came out of the pillar and killed the demon king. This is what the science of Yoga professes that every atom has life and soul and out of which the universe is created. This was the version of Astabakra Muni who first of all gave to the world the idea that 'the universe is the manifestation of the soul'. Before him the idea was just the reverse and people believed that the soul is the manifestation of the universe which was not just and scientific.

In the ladder of God-realization the devotee may extend his belief from matter to man and ultimately to supramental or Param Brahma. He should find out the existence of God everywhere, in himself, in others, in animate and inanimate, as that Supreme Being is omnipresent besides being omnipotent and omniscient.

A sadhak or a seeker of spiritual truth should have this much of knowledge that except in Samadhi there is no other way to union with the infinity or God. All other modes of worship, prayer, offerings, Japa, Tapa, Yaga, Yangya are simply preparation to spirituality. Tantra is the mother of yoga. Tantra helps like a missaile in carrying the sadhak speedily to his destination. Tantra is a double-edged weapon which may be utilized for both: good and evil. The knowledge and use of tantra have been forgotten these days leading to degeneration of spiritual practice in the society.

Mind is the seat of spiritual development which can see, know and perceive. The human mind with its vast capacity is unable to hold and describe the totality of God who is 'abang manasa gochara', means beyond expression through any language and thought. It is just like a sea for one who takes bath and says that he has seen the sea, but at the same time he has not seen it as there are many things in it which he has not seen. Such is the condition of a man who is like a drop in the vast ocean of creation. There is in a drop all the qualities of an ocen as there is in a man all the qualities of God. This inter-relation between a man and God is established only in Samadhi yoga.

A spiritual man is he who has control over his senses. He is free from the bondage of selfishness, anger, greed, ego (pride), partiality and jealousy. Such a man does not see the difference between himself and other men. He always respects the other man's point of view. He sees God in every human being, animal or even in matter. Truth and nonviolence are his way of life. He not only, lives for himself, but also lives for others.

It is, therefore, necessary to analyse the suggestion of Lord Buddha who advised his disciple "Krutadanta" to try to be a good man. What is the nature of a good man. God is good. Goodness is the basic quality in God who desires the wellbeing of all as he is the organizer of the Viswabrahmanda, the universe. One who is good is a godly man. This is the ultimate desire of God, our Supreme Father, Parampita Parameswar. Every father wants that his son should be like him or even better than him. So likes the Parampita Paramatma who's Amrutasya Santan the immortal sons are the human beings. What is goodness then, goodness is that quality that takes us nearer to God who is the embodiment of goodness. One with the quality of goodness always wishes to give and never desires to take. The best of things that a Good man or God wants to give is blessings as all the living beings want a blissful life. They want to live in peace and happiness.

This is the cardinal principle in a folk festival of Kosal region that the Varua after attaining the knowledge and status of a God or Goddess becomes a supernatural creature or being and blesses the people. He tries to answer all their questions and tries to solve their worldly and spiritual problems. He even cures the diseases, blesses the devotees for earthly wealth and blesses them for peace and happiness. In many folk festivals of Kosal region the Baruas maintain silence and do not open their mouth for certain spiritual reasons. However, they move from door to door to bless the people for peace, happiness and prosperity. The Varuas are essentially very good people and, therefore, are godly. The common people find in them the image of gods and goddesses. The reverence on the part of the devotees towards the Varuas in Samadhi brings them to a state of contentment followed by peace and happiness. What else is necessary in spirituality? What else is necessary for a peaceful co-existence in the human society? In that state even the animal world and the plant world are equally respected. The nonliving world is also equally respected for there exists an omnipresent with the essence of life.

Therefore, the folk festivals of Kosal region with their spiritual heroes (Varuas) exhibit the highest kind of spiritual actions and reactions, giving birth to the highest kind of spiritual excellence which should be the eye opener to the mankind.

THE AWAKENING OF KUNDALINI: AN ART AND A SCIENCE

The Siva-Shakti bipolarity of the tantric concept of reality is the basis of the awakening of the Kundalini. She is the Mother Goddess in the microcosm(pinda), whereas Mahakundalini is the same Mother Goddess in the macrocosm (brahmanda). The mouth of the Kundalini closes the Brahmadwara which is the core channel inside the chitrini which is the pathway for the awakened Kundalini for ascent and descent. This Chitrini or Chitra is inside the Vajrini or Vajra. And the latter is inside the susumna. Kundalini is the Maya-Shakti and the

Mahakundalini is the cosmic Maya-Shakti in an individual. The Shakti according to tantra is sentient and active and is the creator, sustainer and absorber of the whole universe. There is no Iswara (God) in the Tantra, but Patanjali's Yoga does not reject Iswara (God), the Mahakundalini at the cosmic level, is the universal shakti; the Kundalini, at the individual level, is also the same shakti.

The dormancy of the Kundalini is not a permanent feature. She can wake up and her arousal can take place in a number of circumstances. There are persons born with awakened Kundalini. Such persons exhibit supra-normal psychic powers since their childhood. Prolonged repetitions of the mantra, if correctly practised, induces the arousal of the sleeping Kundalini. The guru or the priest by way of shaktipata (descent of power) may arouse the kundalini in an individual which instantaneously triggers the awakening of the kundalini. This is how the serpent power (kundalini jagarana) in a Varua of folk festivals of Kosal region is awakened. The priest or purohit or the Deheri remains present physically and by chanting of mantra transmit the spiritual power to the Varua who is influenced already by the beat of drum (the sabdabrahma) in meditation. All the methods of tantra, mantra and yantra also are applied in these festivals to transcend the Varua from concentration, meditation and finally to a state of trance. According to Patanjali yoga the sustained practice of pranayama only can arouse the dormant kundalini.

The ascent of the kundalini is followed by the descent. She departs from Paramasiva and descends through the central channel of susumna. pierces chakra ater chakra and finally reaches the mooladhara where she again coils up and sleeps. This is the exact state of physical and mental condition in a Varua who undergoes through such inexpressible spiritual phenomena unknown to the common men of ignorance about the awakening of the kundalini in such folk festivals. Some readers may raise a question. "How is the Kundalini cycle, involving ascent and descent, important for a person or for mankind? The arousal of the kundalini has important consequences in human mind only to the extent of ten percent of the total. This can be expanded to any level in the range of 10 to 100 by the arousal and proper harness of the kundalini. By its arousal one gains many psychic powers like Clairvoyance, telepathy, precognition etc. one leaves the domain of darkness and enters into that of light. "Tamaso ma jyotirgamaya. Mrityurma Amrutam Gamaya". From a lower level of limited consciousness one reaches a higher level of cosmic consciousness. Everything of one's life undergoes radical transformation-from mental to supra-mental from humane to divine. The arousal of this power would transform the ordinary man into a genius in art and science. Not only the intellectual ability, but also the quality of man would undergo metamorphosis by arousing this latent power. The question about Who am I? Where from I have come? Where shall I go? All can be answered through such awakening. The concept of man becoming God would be actualized by arousing the kundalini power and harnessing it for the good of the entire Cosmos.

CHAPTER FIVE

SOME TYPICAL FOLK FESTIVALS OF KOSAL REGION: WHERE THERE IS NO ANIMAL SACRIFICE

Besides innumerable folk festivals there are some typical folk festivals in Kosal region which are observed with great enthusiasm. Some of them are the 'Dalkhai Yatra', 'Dhunkel Yatra', 'Churakhai Yatra', 'Danda Yatra' etc.

DALKHAI YATRA:

In Dalkhai yatra branches of some trees are worshiped. They are trees of Amla, Bata, Bel, Mandar etc. The deity Dalkhai is a concept which is believed to be in the branches of the trees. The above mentioned trees are very helpful to the human society medically, physically and scientifically. It is true that human beings receive 'Oxygen' from the trees, which is the vital force to their life. Thus the deity in the form of branches of the trees provides such life force to mankind. In fact plants and trees in Indian mythology are considered living deities; 'the Brukshya Devata', the Tree God. As a matter of mark of reverence and devotion to plant kingdom the 'Dalkhai yatra' is observed in the nook and corner of the Kosal region. This is in fact a great human and spiritual tradition preserved by the people of this area since the time immemorial. The observance of the 'Dalkhai yatra' signifies the importance, utility and necessity of the plants and the trees for the survival of the humanity. This folk festival is celebrated mostly by the Adivasis; they live in the districts of Kalahandi, Malkangiri, Rayagada, Nabarangpur, Nuapada, Bolangir, Subarnapur, Bargarh, Jharsuguda, Debgarh, Sambalpur, Sundargarh districts with the name of Kolha, Kondh, Binjhal, Shabara, Kuda, Kutia, Mirdha, Santal, Paraja, Dangaria etc.

This festival is observed on the eight day (Astami tithi) of the sukla pakshya of the Aswina month. This day the non-Adivasi women observe the 'Bhai Juntia' festival which means fasting for the brothers and offering 'pujarchana' with all austerity. They even do not drink a drop of water which is termed as 'nirjala upabasa'. The non-Adivasi women worship the Goddesss Durga this day where as the Adivasi women worship the deity 'Dalkhai', but both the puja upasana are performed with the tantric tradition called 'debri puja'. In this puja the song and music in praise of devi Durga and devi 'Dalkhai' are played. The most important part of dalkhai puja is that the Adivasi men and women dance to the rhythmic tune of the drum beat. The Dalkhai songs are not written, but pass from mouth to mouth since the days of yore and creates vibration in the heart of the listeners. The dalkhai music is enchanting as well as heart throbbing. The song, the dance and the music provide the Adivasi the food for love and merriment for life. They offer the deity birds and animals in sacrifice. They eat their flesh, drink local wine and be merry. This is really the dark side of their lives which make them addicted and render them poor and finally destroy their peace and happiness. Thus their social growth is impaired.

In some villages there are 'Dalkhai Kuthi' or house where such worship take place. In such kuthi the images of Hindu Gods and Goddesses are also found as a mark of Hindu impression on Adivasi religious culture. We see there the picture of Shiva-Parvati, Hanuman, Narada, Varuna, Kubera, Laxmi, Durga, Kali, Saraswati, Budharaja, Bauti, Mauli, Kankali, Samlei, Nilarani, Rahela, Budhi Samlei etc along with their Bahanas; bull, peacock, mouse, tiger, lion etc. The 'Dalkhai' folk festival has intimate relation with the seven (virgin) tantric kumaries of the tantric cult of Kosal region. The dalkhai song chants the name of 'Nitei dhobani', one of the tantric sapta kumaries, popularly known as tantric seven sisters who performed miracles by dint of their tantric skill. The whole folk festival of Dalkhai is associated with the tantric cult which is part and parcel of guhya yoga vidya. As the upasis (women in fast) as well as the Deheri, Dehelia, Barua or Varua also experience the trance or the lower Samadhi according to the Patanjali Yoga Sutra. They are taken by sabda Brahma the sohala varani drum-beat from concentration (dharna) to meditation and from meditation to trance, ecstasy or the lower Samadhi. In that state of trance it is believed that devi (goddess) Dalkhai enters the body of the upasi or the varua. This is for all purposes, purely a yogic (tantric) phenomena, the principles of which are unknown to the common men and women.

DHUNKEL USHA:

The word 'Dhunkel' denotes a musical instrument which is made up of a dhanu (bow) fitted with a string, a Kula (a cleaning instrument for rice made from bamboo stick) and an iron stick to rub on the bow. This musical instrument 'Dhunkel' produces sweet musical sound, sweetest of all the folk musical instruments of Kosal region. This is connected with fertility cult. This festival known as 'Dhunkel Usha' is very popular with the unmarried girls and married women who celebrate this festival for good husbands and for obtaining good children. For celebrating the folk festival of 'Dhunkel' we see dhunkel usha kuthi in the villages. Even in the town of Sonepur, Binka, Tarva and many other township of Kosal region we used to find dhunkel usha kuthis and now extinct, bidding goodbye to a great spiritual and cultural tradition.

From my experience in the fifties and early part of sixties the virgins and the married women used to gather in such kuthis at Sonepur. They sit in meditating posture and when the dhunkel musical instrument starts playing and the devotional song chanted by the musician preferably an old man, the women baruas or varuas start trembling and then dance to the tune of 'Dhunkel'. Her hair disheveled, her cloth in disarray she dances frantically in ecstasy after the schedule time frame in meditation. The women varuas observe all austerity of puja and fasting. The devotional songs are mostly in praise of Lord Shiva and Parvati and the song tells the story of one princess called Rahela the daughter of the king of Kosal and his wife queen Leelavati. Princess Rahela at the age of seven wanted to perform 'Dalkhai' puja which was denied by her parents and relatives. In grief Rahela committed suicide at Nitai Dhobani tutha. When searched after by her near and dear ones she was found playing with the seven tantric sisters.

Her relatives prayed for her life. The tantric seven siddha kumaris gave back Rahela, but on condition that she would be allowed to observe Dalkhai puja and from that period onward Dalkhai puja attained the form of a folk festival as the legend goes. The tradition continues till today as an inseparable part of the Kosli culture in the form of dance, drama, music and song.

CHURAKHAI YATRA:

Churakhai or chudakhai yatra of Risband in Boudh district of Kosal region is famous for its licentiousness and erotic appeal. The participatnts in this folk festival chant obscene songs while marching with the black and white umbrella (chhatar) the symbol of energy (shakti) and peace (shanti). They also carry with them earthen symbols of sexual organs. This folk festival is purely tribal in nature and based on tantric cult where sex is not taboo. The name of the village Risban is derived from the word 'Rusibandh' means bound by saints and sages. The Adivasi saints were adept in the art of tantric yoga culture as history goes. They were successful in establishing cultural and spiritual tradition of high order which aim at strict discipline of the society. The festival aims at the idea of transforming the sexual energy into kinetic energy or creative energy which is the basic object of all religions. The same principle is adopted in the car festival of Lord Jagannath at Puri. By singing obscene songs, the 'Dahukas' try to create physical energy in devotees for smooth motion of the chariot. Due to such influence of the spiritual heads the Adivasis even today live in a world of spirit. They invite the spirit in the body of a varua and talk to the spirit and do according to the advice of the spirit during trance or the Lower Samadhi of the varua which is an important part of the yogic excellence based on scientific principles propounded by

Maharshi Patanjali in his text 'Yoga Sutra'.

Through the practice of Samayama (dharana, dhyana and Samadhi) the Adivasis try to find all the answers to their questions and all the solutions to their problems. This idea is more predominant among Adivasi people who establish a temple in their own house and consider the same a shrine of heavenly spirit which is a part of sophisticated Adivasi (tribal) culture.

The churakhai yatra begins on the last Thursday of the month of Margashira and ends on the next Thursday. Thus this folk festival runs for long eight days. The festival takes place in the temple of village Risban where goddess Churakhai is enshrined. Churakhai is the local name of goddess Maheswari. A legend goes that two fishermen (keuta) named Lui and Beji first of all started the puja of churakhai which was later supported by the gauntia (headman) of the village who was an Adivasi. At the beginning a water pot (Kalasi) and two golden sticks were worshipped as the symbol of goddess Maheswari (churakhai). By the grace of goddess Maheswari there appeared a lingam which was worshipped. This has given rise to the tradition of fertility cult in association of both linga and yoni. The goddess is named churakhai as the main Prasad which is offered to her is Chuda or chura means parched rice. About fifty-two villages used to take part in this unique folk festival. The Kalasi (water pot) and the chhatar (umbrella) are taken in procession with a group of musicians, who used to play dhol, nisan, tasa, mahuri etc. The procession marches to a nearby dangar (hillock) where a kalasi (water pot) is kept earlier. The kalasi is tied with plantain leaf filled with water, curd and arua rice by the Deheri, the worshipper. While the kalasi and chhatar are taken to the villages, the people welcome them and make arrangements for dance and music. The kalasi and chhatar move round the villages for long seven days and at last the chhatars are kept closed in two earthen pots (handi) and the kalasi is worshiped in the temple as goddess Maheswari. At this time the kalasi of the previous year is opened which indicates the fortune (good or evil) for the year in accordance with the content of the water in the pot.

Churakhai yatra is also observed at Marjakud of Boudh on the same day where women folk sing obscene songs and men keep quiet, but at Risban the women remain silent while the men sing obscene songs. It is believed that eating of Simba and Mahula (mahua flower) is forbidden before churakhai yatra with the intention to allow the fruits to ripe and become edible which is scientific. This idea is applied to the gundikhai yatra to protect the mango fruits when they are not ripe.

There is tradition of animal sacrifice before the goddess churakhai in this churakhai yatra which seems to be a degeneration of the spiritual culture, from churakhai to the blood sucker of innocent animals. This change in tradition is due to the ignorance of the people who for their selfish attitude have started sacrificing the animals instead of sacrificing their own ego and sacrificing their own blood to appease the God or Goddess.

DANDA YATRA:

Danda yatra is another typical folk festival of Kosal region the origin of which can be dated back to the $5^{th}/6^{th}$ century B.C. to the $5^{th}/6^{th}$ century A.D. while a very developed human civilization flourished on the banks of the river Mahanadi and the Tel. Sonepur being situated at the confluence of three rivers: the Mahanadi, the Tel and the Karpura river ultimately became the epicenter of the said civilization. At that time, a lot of cultural tradition developed in the field of food, shelter, cloth, agriculture, industries along with the spiritual and religious practices. We come across a lot of food items such as chaulbara, chakapitha, baragulia, papchi, gudbara, mahufena, atkali, gambhari pitha, sarsatia, dantiri khaja, murhiladu, lialadu, janjala ladu, mekaladu etc. The invention of Tye and Dye cloth (ikat) can be traced to that period and Sonepur has been the centre of that art of weaving even today. The Sonepuri or Subarnapuri art of weaving has been adjudged as the best by the research scholars of national and international repute. In the matter of shelter the concept of 'dhabaghar' 'first floor' made up of wood, bamboo, mud and straw is a great contiribution of the Kosal region to mankind. The professors and scholars from the Pune University under the leadership of Dr.H.S.Sankhalia had thrown light about the said civilization. Among the scholars were Dr.Asok Marathe, Dr.Ansari and Surveyor Mr.Kulkarni. The author along with Dr.N.K.Sahu, Ex-vice chancellor of Sambalpur University, Dr.P.M.Nayak, ex-principal of Sonepur college was associated with the project of archeological excavation at the confluence near Sonepur town in 1980.

It is believed that during that period from $5^{th}/6^{th}$ century B.C. to $5^{th}/6^{th}$ century A.D. the danda yatra flourished as a Buddhist folk festival where according to the Bajrayanists the human male sexual organ is considered 'Bajra', 'Linga' and that of female sexual organ as 'Lotus', 'Yoni'. The concept of linga and yoni later considered to be a part of Shaiba ritual in which the worship of Linga and Yoni prevailed. The Somavansi kings who ruled over their empire from Sonepur were basically ardent devotees of Lord Shiva and Parvati. Therefore, as a mark of their devotion to Lord Shiva they had built Kosaleswar temple at Baidyanath and Kapileswar temple at Charda near Binika. Sonepur reflects the sweet assimilation of the Shakta, Shaiva and Baishnava cult where we find the temples of asta Chandi, asta Sambhu and asta Vishnu. It is the citadel of Buddhist vajrayana Tantra yoga propounded by the philosopher king Indrabhuti and also the citadel of the Buddhist Sahajayana Tantra Yoga propounded by his sister Bhagavati Laxmikara. We see the principles of both vajrayana tantra and sahajayana tantra practised in the danda yatra of Kosal region. Later both Shaibite and Vaishanabite themes have been introduced to suit the need and taste of the viewers as well as the performers. The whole danda yatra is associated with fertility cult and has developed in course of time as a strong and very effective spiritual tradition giving birth to excellent literary and musical tradition with astounding performing art of dance, drama and music under the open sky.

The foundation of danda yatra is tantra and yoga around which this literary musical and dramatic tradition has evolved. The literary tradition has not been captured through pen and paper, but has passed from mouth to mouth and mind to mind. This yatra has been able to create hundreds of poetic, dramatic and musical genius.

Undoubtedly, the origin of danda yatra is the panchara ilaka means Panchara area, situated between Baunsuni and Manamunda of Boudh district which once upon a time belonged to Sonepur ex-state. The word 'danda' which means sticks is derived from four 'dandas' which are worshipped in this festival as the symbol of lord Shiva. Each danda is ten fingers long (dasa angula) before the beginning of danda yatra those four sticks of the shape and size of Linga are carried in a special ritual and after that all the four sticks (danda) are set on fire. This is called danda jinaiba or bringing the danda to life. From beginning to the end of this festival these four dandas are very important and indispensible. These 'dandas' play very vital role and carry with them ten goddesses, prava, thirteen Bhoktas, musicians etc. and about 30-40 participants move from place to place for long thirteen days, maximum 21 days. The festival starts from the seventheenth day of Chaitra and ends on the vishuva sankranti or pana sankranti of Vaisakha. The month of Chaitra is marked by the shakta devotees as the month of the goddess (devi). Irrespective of caste and creed the people are associated with this folk festival. Mostly they belong to the lower strata of the society, but in celebration of the festival there remains no caste discrimination. The 'danda yatra' is basically a folk festival observed in pomp and ceremony by the tribal people which has been adopted by the non-tribals as a festival of faith and spiritual tradition. It is founded on tribal culture. It is surprising that animal sacrifice is completely forbidden in this festival following the siddha yogic principle of Gorakshyanath. In place of animal a sweet (pitha prepared from rice and biri) is offered to the deity as a matter of sacrifice.

The 'Veenakar' as lord Shiva and 'Veenakaruni or Vinakariani' as Goddess Parvati appear on the stage and sing the prayer to lord Ganesh. The veenakar plays the pivotal role in the danda yatra. The other thirteen voktas or devotees are the thirteen sons of thirteen sages of Hindu mythology, viz, vinayaka, chanda, prachanda, munda, vrugu, vrukuti, nandi, agnishatra, manivadra, mukunda, bhimanka, mahakala and mantry Gyanasena. The supandita or the knowledgeable Trikalangya is the first patavokta of danda yatra. Vinayaka and chanda hold the fire danda.

Prachanda and munda hold the prava of Goddess Kali. Nandi Vrukuti and Agnishatra become the Shavara and Shavaruni. Manivadra and Veenakara act as the watchmen of the storehouse, Veemanka and Mahakala become the dagara, Mukunda acts as administrator and Bhrugu accomplishes the role of pata dhulia or main musician who beat the drum (dhola) and thus spread the Shaiva cult. People of sixtyfour pataka (caste and creed) take part-in this folk festival which by its popularity has been able to defeat the importance of Buddhist religion which was spreading like wild fire. The danda yatra is believed to have been performed in all ages (yuga) satya, tretaya, dwapara and kali and thus proves its primitive and ancient nature. There are innumerable legends as regards the origin and beginning of danda yatra. It is also called Shiva yatra after the name of lord Shiva. Lord Shiva is the presiding deity of the danda voktas.

Many scholars term danda yatra as danda nata. Nata means drama. It is in fact, not a mere drama or enactment, but the enactment follows the spiritual tradition that is so important to hold the human society intact. This is not meant for musical or dramatic or even literary development, it is really meant for spiritual development. Like any other folk festivals of Kosal region the dance, drama, song, music and literature have followed the footsteps of spiritual development. Here Swami Vivekananda's statement that- 'Spiritual development is the only development' holds good and all other development naturally follow the spiritual development. The spiritual development establishes a natural selfdiscipline which helps speedy development in all the fields of life. In fact the society, where the danda yatra originated, enjoyed all round prosperity at that time.

In the danda yatra the shakta pramoda vadya tattwa, sohala varani badya or shoal kathi vadya is played and the man holding prava enters the state of trance while dancing to the tune of the music played. Unlike other folk festivals of Kosal region the prava man starts dancing and then with the effect of music enters into trance or the lower Samadhi when it is believed that God or Goddess entered the body of the same man dancing with prava.

The common factor in all the three cults: Shakta, Shaiva and Baishnava is fertility where the concept of sex is predominant. There are two types of danda seen now-a-days: The sohala suanga and the Leela danda or pratham vet or first meeting. The sohala suanga danda is original and primary which is based on the sakta and shaiva cult and the Leela danda is based on the theme of Radha Krishna love story. The sohala suanga danda yatra is still prevalent in the Boudh and Kandhomal districts whereas Leela danda played mostly in the Subarnapur and Bolangir districts. Ofcourse sohala suanga danda is also celebrated in some parts of both Bolangir and Subarnapur districts. The Leela danda has also been invented on the soil of Sonepur the modern name of which is Subarnapur in consonance with its historical name. The Chauhan rulers were Baishanabites who built so many temples like vitri Gopaljee, Bada Gopaljee, Nrusinghnath or Gundicha temple, Sri Jagannath temple, Gopinath temple, Dadhibamana temple, Brundavana Bihari temple at Sonepur town and under the royal patronage Jagannath temples were built almost in every village of ex-state of Sonepur. This is because of a shift from the shakta and shaiva cult of the Chauhan rulers to Vaishnava cult. There is no doubt that danda yatra plays an important role in moulding the spiritual and social life of the people of Kosal region. This tradition has spread to other parts of Odisha and outside also. We see sohala suanga danda in the districts of Ganjam. Gajapati, Keonjhar, Mayurbhanj etc. and in the state of Assam and West Bengal danda yatra is also performed.

The danda yatra can be divided into seven parts; bata barana, bana danda, dhuli danda, pani danda, agni danda, danduali and suanga. Bata barana means inviting the deity and the devotees for danda yatra by the jajaman, the man interested to organize danda yatra. Bana danda means the Bhoktas take shelter under a mango grove or near a pond or river after being invited. Dhuli danda is performed on the village road under the scorching heat of the sun. Here the bhoktas exhibit the agricultural performance. Dhuli danda is based on the physical exercise and spiritual and yogic penance (tapa). At this time the 'bhoktas' chant 'Kala Rudramani Ki Bhaje'. After 'dhuli danda' the 'Bhoktas' observe pani danda in the evening, in which they enshrine the Shiva linga with thirteen handfuls of sand. They worship the Chhatra, Bairakha, Rudrakali. After that they rub two pieces of wood and set the four dandas (lingam) on fire. After 'pani danda' the bhoktas perform 'agni danda' at night and carry the dandas in fire from house to house by sprinkling dhupa, jhuna on the fire and the scene inspires awe and fear among the people with the heart-throbbing dance and music.

Danduali means all the 'Bhokatas' in their appointed attire who enter the open air stage dancing in tune with the 'mahuri'. After that 'Sohala suanga' the main drama of danda yatra is enacted with full enthusiasm. There are sixteen (sohala) suangas means sixteen different characters and only the 'Baidhana' has no pair, but all other fifteen pairs have duet role play. They are (1) Hadi-Hadiani, (2) for holding the danda and jhuna khela 2 persons, (3)

Parava-Paravani (4) Ishwar-Parvati (5) Chadheya-Chadheyani (6) Fakira-Fakirani (7) Nabchhanka-Nabchhanki (8) Shali-Vinoi (9) Kela-Keluni (10) Bhalua-Bhaluani (11) Jogi-Jogiani (12) Diara-Bhauja (13) Baidhana (14) Shavara-Shavaruni (15) Patra Sahura-Patra Sahurani (16) Veenakar-Veenakaruni.

The danda nata or danda dance is a divine dance derived from the Shiva Tandava nrutya. This is one of the main folk festivals of Kosal region as well as the state of Odisha. In this festival the Bhoktas undergo severe penance which marks a sense of deep devotion for God Shiva. Fasting in austerity, control of passion are the prime requisites of this festival. The deep sense of spirituality accompanied by dance, drama and music make this folk festival the best of all and provide the common people a platform for sublime enjoyment and entertainment. They look forward to this grand folk festival for the whole life. Achandala Brahmana and abala-brudhabanita wait very eagerly to witness this celebration for long thirteen days and forget the sweating heat of summer. We find in the writing of Bhikari Charan Das in 'Danda falashruti'.

"Sama drustire chanhile jagata
Hoi pariba se Shivanka bhakta".

The stanza reminds us about the definition of yoga in Srimad Bhagavat Geeta, "Samatwam yoga uchyate" which confirms the meaning of the stanza composed by the poet Bhikari Charan Das. The number thirteen which is considered inauspicious in Christian culture is considered auspicious in danda yatra. The thirteen Bhoktas (devotees) propagate in thirteen villages thirteen different messages of social service and social reforms for long thirteen days. The danda yatra is a unique folk festival of Kosal region which demands patronage from the public and the administration.

CHAPTER SIX

YOGA IN INDIAN CULTURE AND KOSAL REGION

Ever since the dawn of civilization man has been searching for eternal peace and happiness. All our culture, religion and scriptures have centered round this eternal peace and happiness. For this eternal peace Yogeswar Lord Krishna had taught Arjuna the principles of Yoga in Srimad Bhagabat Geeta five thousand years ago. Geeta teaches mankind the essence of the principle of nonattachment. After two thousand and five hundred years of Mahabharata it was Maharshi Patanjali of Aryan Age who propounded the practical aspects of yoga through Asthanga Yoga: Yama, Niyama, Asana, Pranayama, Pratyahara, Dharana, Dhyana and Samadhi. There was time when Astanga Yoga was a way of life for Indians. Every citizen led a yogic life which contributed to the development of the society. The truth about it could be realized from the folk festivals of Kosal region which continued for several hundred years. It is again after two thousand and five hundred years of Maharshi Patanjali, Maharshi Sri Aurobinda could bring down the supramental into his body and said, "True spirituality starts after Samadhi". In 1956 in the "World Federation of Mental Health" the Nobel Laureate Julien Huxley said, "The Western scientists should learn from their Estern counterpart the art of controlling breath and entering trance." This again means yoga is nothing but pure science and thus spirituality is nothing but the science of sciences. It is through this science of yoga one can enter into the state of trance, the Lower Samadhi. In this state of Samadhi union of Atma with the Paramatma is possible. It is called by Sri Aurobinda the Jeebanmukti, which means salvation in present life. It is only in the state of Samadhi that the Supramental descends. The descendence of the supramental is possible only in the state of Samadhi. The state of Samadhi is based on certain scientific principles with some precise mathematical formula which is worked out in the 'Bali Yatra' and 'Maheswari Yatra' of Subarnapur and many other such festivals in different parts of Kosal Region, where there is Varua Tattwa.

Subarnapur is a tiny town of temples in Koshal region. Once upon a time this town was the capital city of erstwhile Kosal Empire. There are one hundred and eight temples including the temples of Asta Chandi, Asta Shiva and Asta Vishnu. The town is situated on the holy confluence of the rivers the Mahanadi, the Tel and the Karpura (hidden). It is at this place that the most enchanting spiritual phenomenon occurs where the illiterate farmer and labour class people through "Sabda Brahma", the beats of drum known as "Sohala Varani", are taken from meditation to the lower Samadhi, the state of trance. The Sabda Brahma or Sohala Varani drum beats are based on Sakta Pramoda Badya Tattwa composed by one Adivasi Saint named Sonar Sang village Rahela (Rohilaka) of Subarnapur district. The sixteen different types of drum-beats symbolize the sixteen different types of state of body and mind of the Varua passing through the state of varani to chhadni. The drum-beats eclipse the mind of the Varua and helps him in pratyahara and dharana (concentration). The concentration leads to meditation and finally to state of Trance (Samadhi).

The lower Samadhi according to the book "Patanjali Yoga Sutra" written by two authors of international reputation on yoga, Swami Pravabananda Saraswati and Christopher Isherwood where they have said that if the mind is concentrated on one point for 12 seconds it is concentration, if that concentration prolongs for 2 minutes and 24 seconds that becomes meditation. If that meditation prolongs for 28 minutes and 48 seconds that becomes lower Samadhi. If that lower Samadhi continues for 5 hours 45 minutes and 36 seconds that becomes the "Nirbikalpa Samadhi" in which the transmigration of soul is possible. In Subarnapur Bali Yatra and Maheswari Yatra the principles of lower Samadhi are followed. The same principles are also followed in the Kalasi yatra of Charda, Dhunkel Usha and Dalkhai Yatra of many places, Chattar yatra of Bhawanipatna, Patakhanda yatra of Jarasingha, Kumari Sadhana yatra of Deogarh, Maheswari yatra of Kirabahal, Dwarasenhi yatra of Sindhekela, Chudakhai yatra of Risban, Budhidokra yatra and Kantakuanri yatra of Banei, Samalei yatra of Tushra, Kanavainro yatra of Nuapada, Danda yatra of Boudh and Subarnapur, Lankeswari yatra and Budhima yatra of Subarnapur etc. where Varua is the hero and where Sakta Pramoda Badya Tattwa plays its part.

In the lower Samadhi the spirit is aroused in the body of the 'Varua the man in meditation, and at this stage his mind and body go from voluntariness to involuntariness.

He loses the sense of pain and pleasure, vice and virtue, foe and friend, falsehood and truth and there manifest seven symptoms in his body and mind. They are Spandan (tremor), Ghurni (zyration), Udvav (levitation), Ananda (elation), Nidra (drowsiness), Murchha (sooning) and Jagruti (awakening) as Swami Shivananda writes in his book "The Mind, its mystery and control", it is the awakening of the mind which is the most important and which is termed by Maharshi Patanjali as 'Tad Jaya Pragyan Lokah'. By this the power of the mind is increased manifold and the man in trance can see the unseen and know the unknown. He or she speaks some language quite alien to him or her and sometimes forecasts the past, future and present. It is through this process the spirit or the supramental descends down the body of the Varua. Then he is adorned like a God or Goddess with Vermilion on his forehead and garlands of china-rose on the neck and then he marches ahead into the society to bless the people. The people offer him puja with great reverence. In the Bali yatra cartload of Samidha and pure cow ghee were burnt in homa and yajna in early days. In both Bali yatra and Maheswari yatra of Subarnapur there are specific tests for trance. The Varua in a state of trance walks on fire, sits on the thorny swing, rubs on the body the Indian Nettle leaves and sometimes even drinks fresh raw blood from the severed trunk of animals. In the Bali yatra and Maheswari yatra of Subarnapur all the principles of Yantra, Mantra and Tantra are adopted to take the Varua from the state of meditation to the state of Samadhi. The Purohita or the priest is the most important person in this spiritual action who controls the activities of the Varua being assisted by four associates known as Chargharias. Those who hold Chhatar (umbrella) are known as chhatrias. Those who hold the torches or the masal are known as masaltis. Thus people from all classes 'Achandala brahmana' including the king of the princely state were associated with this Bali yatra. This Yatra is celebrated in the most spiritual and festive mood in royal regalia. This festival of sacrifice, which means the sacrifice of ego and not the sacrifice of animal, takes place in several temples of goddesses at Subarnapur from the New Moon Day (Mahalaya) to the next day of Full Moon (Purnima) of the month of Aswina every year. Its beginning can be dated back to the days of Lord Parshuram the Aryan hero who performed yajna near the confluence at Subarnapur which is the epicenter of culture of Odisha. That sacred place of yajna is popularly known as Khaulgad wherefrom mysterious soil is brought out by a Varua on the fifth day of Ashwina Suklapakshya. It is believed that due to the Ashwamedha yajna of Parashuram the soil of that hole, known as Biramurchha garta, is sanctified by chemical reactions and helps the Varua in meditation.

Sacrifice in Bali Yatra of Subarnapur does not mean the sacrifice of animal, but if means the sacrifice of the self, the sacrifice of ego which is the cardinal principle of yoga. The Varuas belong to Sakama a nearby village of Subarnapur town. They lead a pious and peaceful life. Their wives and family members are extremely happy for this kind of spiritual performance and realization. Now this festival has degenerated into an act of animal sacrifice. It may be noted that all the 16 days of Bali yatra sacrifice of animals does not take place and in Maheswari yatra animal sacrifice does not take place at all. With the passage of time the sacrifice of the self has turned into sacrifice of the other self which finally culminated in human sacrifice which scarcely took place in this bali yatra during the rule of Chauhans long before independence. The popularity of Subarnapur Bali yatra can attain international height by exposing more and more of its yogic excellence and less and less of animal sacrifice. Will the public understand the subtle scientific principles of spirituality and yoga and stop unnecessary and unethical sacrifice of innocent animals, for the purpose of attaining spiritual excellence and cherish God's blessings? In fact the people of Kosal region, have suffered untold misery due to lack of faith in their established culture and tradition. There is spiritual and cultural degeneration in every sphere of life. One need not be surprised to learn that the people of the Kosal region have become the poorest people in the whole world. That they have become self-centered, indolent and instead of sacrificing their ego, they have started sacrificing the animals in spiritual festivals which might have brought them the all round downfall by way of the curse of the gods and goddesses. The age-old festivals of Kosal region are pregnant with the scientific principles of yoga which are gradually becoming very popular with the people of the whole world. If the festivals are revived to the taste of the outsiders then tourists will rush to this region to witness such fantastic spiritual performance. Thus the economic and social problems of the people of this area can be solved.

The Bali yatra of Subarnapur is unique of its kind and unparalleled in the whole world. No such festival is ever celebrated in any part of the world at any point of time in such a grand manner with the involvement of so many people, so many places and so much time. The Bali yatra of Subarnapur demands recognition of highest order, but as ill luck would have it the local intelligentsia have also no knowledge of its gravity and grandeur. Like the musk deer, with the musk (Kasturi) in its navel, which searches after its fragrance outside frantically, the people also search after their key to development outside their spiritual excellence. The people of Kosal region have been thoroughly exploited by politicians and bureaucrats. The development of their language, culture, spirit have been seriously affected. This has degraded their economic and social life. They are leading a miserable life under pressure and suffering due to unpardonable crime of regional imbalance. It is high time that they stood up and agitated for their own existence and tried to straighten their cultural and linguistic problems by way of reviving the traditional spiritual folk-festivals where their secret of real uplift lies.

CHAPTER SEVEN

ANIMAL SACRIFICE : CAUSE OF EARTHQUAKE AND TSUNAMI

"Fools rush in where angels fear to tread". The selfish and cruel hearted foolish people do not know what sin they commit by killing the cows mercilessly to eat their flesh. It is as bad as eating one's mother's flesh. Why it is so, a scientific view point is discussed in this chapter.

Recently, three Indian scientists of Delhi University namely Madan Mohan Bajaj, Mohammad Sayed Ibrahim and Bijayraj Singh have discovered that frequent earthquakes are taking place because of excessive killing of animals, specially the cows. Their theory is named BIS after the first letter of their names. In this BIS theory they have analysed that the painful sound 'ah!' created by the animals at the moment of dying causes vibration in the ethereal strata of the world which ultimately causes earthquake. They have tried to prove the effect of such sorrowful sound in a scientific condition. They have carried out their experiment in Russia and received applause from the foreign scientists.

It is a fact that the universe is created out of the panchamahabhuta (elements): Khiti, ap, teja, marut and byoma (earth, water, fire, air and ether). All the five elements are connected to one another. A tremor in one may cause tremor in other elements. This is purely scientific. According to the law of motion every action has its equal and opposite reaction. It is also naturally true that a bad action has its equal and opposite bad reaction. Killing itself is a violent act. The sound of 'ah!' produced by the animals before death is terrifying. In the forest the sound of the lion and the tiger and that of the cow in the midst of human habitation is most loud and vibrant. It is heart-rending. The dreadful death sound of cows creates a tremendous vibration. Such vibration affects the earth causing earthquake in course of time.

This is the reason for which cow slaughter is forbidden in our scriptures. Even Jogeswar Lord Krishna has stated this theory of earthquake in the Mahabharata days. One day Arjuna saw tears rolling down the cheeks of Lord Krishna. Arjuna was stupefied and asked humbly the reason of such tears. Lord Krishna replied that He is feeling extreme pain in his heart of hearts seeing the merciless killing of cows in the Kaliyuga and on account of the Ha Maa! sound of the cows there would be terrific earthquake for which the human race will be in great turbulence. That is why tears roll down from my eyes seeing the untold suffering of mankind in Kaliyuga, said Lord Krishna. Arjuna was moved by the words of Lord Krishna and he vowed to protect the cows being born in Kaliyuga.

On the other hand the cow has been described as Gomata (mother cow) in ancient scriptures. The description is not unfounded. It is based on social and biological truth. Next to our own mother who has given us birth, it is cow alone who serves the purpose of second mother for our whole life. Our own mother feeds us with milk for only some months, but we take milk and milk products from the cow for the whole life. A cow even after her death gives us her skin, bone, horn etc. which come to our use.

The cow gives us cowdung which is adjudged as the best manure and out of her urine is prepared very valuable medicines. Gojharan is a very cheap but popular ayurvedic medicine which cures all types of stomach diseases and is useful in skin diseases, arthritis, bodyache, headache, liver and kidney ailment. The cow is the best domestic animal and considered a symbol of prosperity. There is no other animal as useful as the cow.

Eating beef is a part of the non-vegetarian food item. It satisfies the flesheating people who do not consider cow a respectable animal as Gomata. It is not only irreligious but also unwise to kill cows for beef. It is most unscientific too. If the scientific cause of earthquake is known to the people they will not like to eat beef anymore and thereby the cow race will be saved and can be utilized for the prosperity of mankind.

The protection of the cows entails a spiritual thinking. How can one kill someone who gives so much for prosperity in life? Only such a person can kill who is insensible and devoid of scientific knowledge. The cow is the best creation of God in the animal world. It is created for the need for good food for mankind. Lord Krishna, for that reason, laid utmost importance to the cow and to teach a lesson to the insensible man He took birth and was fostered by the cowherd king Nanda and queen Yosada. His childhood days were spent in the midst of the cowherd boys and cows. He was deeply associated with the milk and milk product like curd, butter etc. According to the World Health Organization of United Nations curd is the best food in the world. According to the same WHO Indian way of life is the best in the world. Indian culture is basically Krishna (cult) culture.

There is an interesting episode in the Srimat Bhagabatam where Lord Krishna requested Lord Shiva for two blessings. The first is, I shall eat abundant Khir (sweet prepared of rice and milk) and the second, I shall feed people with plenty of Khir. From this episode we learn how keen was Lord Krishna in eating and feeding such sweet items prepared from cow milk.

The world is slowly, but steadily tilting towards vegetarianism. Due to wrong food habit, lack of exercise and food adulteration, people are suffering from many diseases. The change of food habit from non-vegetarian to vegetarian is gaining popularity in foreign countries like Germany, USA, England and other European countries. Non-vegetarian foodstuffs are causing unknown diseases like Anthrax, Bird-flue and Swine-flue etc. which are contagious and spread like an epidemic. Therefore, more educated people in foregn countries quickly change their habit to escape health hazards. It may be noted that in Germany 60% of people take vegetarian diet. One of the author's friends Mr. Martin Brand, an archeologist, revealed this fact and said that the German scientists have developed ten improved (high-breed) varieties of beans in their country whereas in India we have been able to develop only three to four varieties. Prof. Joana Williams of Southeast Asian Art Department of California University, another personal friend of the author, who herself turned to be a vegetarian said that she changed her food habit because of her affection for her son and devotion to Lord Jagannath who are strict vegetarians. For the bio-friendly fruits and vegetables cows have a great role to play. The chemical fertilizers and pesticides help to produce more quantity of agricultural produce, but they are deadly so far as their quality is concerned and they produce fatal diseases like cancer, and other stomach and cardiac diseases. The cow can change the entire bio-diversity of the world and can provide healthy food habits to the people.

It is astonishing that innumerable animals and birds are sacrificed every year in folk festivals of Kosal region. Sacrifice of animals can never be called a spiritual act. This is nothing, but degeneration of spirituality and ultimately is the cause of earthquake and Tsunami according to the BIS theory. Once the animal sacrifice is stopped in Kosal region the place will change from hell to heaven and people from all over the world will throng to this region to witness the spectacular spiritual events that take place through yogic performance in the folk festivals. Even though cruelty to animal is forbidden in law of the land the ignorant and self seeking people of Kosal region forget the true ways to appease their gods and goddesses. That is why they are less blessed and less prospered. It is true that the craze for eating flesh has caused large-scale animals acrifice in the folk festivals of Kosal region. The craze becomes unethical when it concerns the gods and goddesses and their worship. That is why the curse on the people of Kosal region. That is why their economic, social and spiritual degradation.

CHAPTER EIGHT

GOD REALIZATION DURING FOLK FESTIVALS OF KOSAL REGION

Many things have been stated in scriptures of all religions about salvation. The idea of salvation has also been contradicted and the existence of either soul (atman) or God (Paramatman) has been denied by some schools of thoughts. The non-believers (atheists) believe that God is the creation of the mind of man, but they cannot answer the question as to who is the creator of man. They also cannot say anything about the motive force behind the creation. Lord Krishna has said in one sentence to Arjuna- "What will you gain by knowing all this in detail, Arjuna? Suffice it to say that I stand holding this entire universe by a spark of My yogic power".

"God is not a mere concept. He is not imaginary. He is only the Real who never ceases to be. It needs knowledge to perceive Him. We cannot see oxygen and hydrogen, but when they combine in exact proportion H_2O, we get water which we can see. The same is the quality of God whom we cannot see, but can perceive through exact knowledge. He is one and the same and is only called by different names such as Parameswara, Paramatma, Brahma, Purosottama, Allah, God, Khuda etc. The universe consists of two substances: the spiritual and the material. They are also known as Purusha (spirit) and Prakriti (matter). The spirit has been further sub-divided as individual soul (jeebatma) and the Universal Soul (Paramatma), the former being the part and parcel of the latter. The individual souls are numerous whereas the universal soul is one". God is formless, but can take form according to the desire of the devotee. Such were the devotees like Surdas, Tulsidas, Tukaram, Narasi, Chaitanya, Mirabai, Ramkrishna who could see God in their desired form. The medium of their desire is love. Sage Patanjali, too, says in his "Aphorisms on Yoga", "Repetition of the names of one's beloved Deity induces Him to appear in person". Just as a yogi who has completely mastered his will is able to visualize whatever he likes to have before his eyes. The Lord manifests before his devotee who is absorbed in His love. The Vision is possible through satsang, remembrance of God, purity of heart and intense longing to see God. For this one should fix his whole attention on God with full concentration (dharana). Such dharana is possible only with a perfect pratyahara (rejection) of all other things (neti, neti or not this, not this). The singleminded devotion is called Radha Bhava. Bhava is better than puja, aradhana, yoga, yaga, yajna, japa etc. and of all bhavas the Radha Bhava is the best. When Uddhava told the gopis that they should not hanker after His body which is temporal and transitory, they should worship his Nirakara parambrahma roopa, the gopis said it is foolish to hanker after the formless roopa of Krishna. Then he wanted to see the condition of Radha Rani and found her sitting in seclusion, tears rolling down her cheeks. Uddhav thought that Radha was shedding tears perhaps due to separation from Krishna. But Radha said, “Uddhava, are you not able to see that my Lord Krishna is sitting beside me?” At this the inner eyes of Uddhav were opened. He could see Lord Krishna was sitting by the side of Radha. This is the strength of Radha Bhaba in a nutshell.

To obtain a glimpse of God one has to renounce woman, wealth and all worldly pleasures, even pleasures of the sense organs. This is possible only on the part of a yogi in the true sense of the term. A yogi believes in jeevanmukti (liberation in this life). He believes in the present. This moment, this life is the most important for him. He acquires knowledge of the past, present and future, but lives in the present.

Selfsacrifice and sacrifice of the ego is the prime requisite in God realization. It is said that on one side of the coin there is ego and on the other side there is God. By meditation on the self (atma) a yogi will reach the abode of Samadhi (absorption) and Samadhi will bring emancipation. For a successful meditation one has to master the art of concentration (dharana). The concentration should be on Him who dwells in the heart of hearts of every man and woman. In meditation the subtle mind in the form of atma (soul) descends down and settles in the heart. It is a matter of selfrealization. It is, therefore, said by Rishi Yaganvalka “Atma Hrutpratishtham” means the soul is established in the heart. It means the heart is the shrine of the soul. It is also believed and found to be true that the heart (antahkarana) is the shrine of the Paramatma, the Universal Soul or God. Therefore, it clearly means that the union of the Individual Soul (jeevatma) and the Universal Soul (Paramatma) takes place in the heart of the meditator. This union of both individual soul and universal soul takes place only in the state of Samadhi (absorption). A yogi can stay in that state of Samadhi at any time according to his sweet will. This is achieved by way of practice. Such practice alone makes a yogi perfect. Then the yogi is liberated even in his life time and this is called jeevanmukti.

All pervasiveness of God proves that He is present everywhere. He is found hidden like ghee in butter and butter in milk. To get ghee one has to heat the milk, get the butter and heat the butter again to get the ghee. Likewise to obtain God one has to undergo such penance, burn and burn to get pure gold, God.

Meditation on the form of the Lord with full faith may lead to God realization. The practice of seeing infinite forms of the world as only so many manifestations of the same God may also lead to God realization. The practice of truth in thought, word and action is bound to lead to God realization. The practice of concentration on the Nada-Brahma or Sabda-Brahma may ultimately lead to God realization. God realization will be easy to attain even by recognizing life-breath as Brahma and the sound emanating therefrom as the name of the Brahma. Thus God may be realized even by recognizing breath to be Brahma. The outgoing and ingoing breath produces the sound 'Soham' which means "That (God) I am. Any such practice if pursued with a selfish motive may lead to fulfilment of one's selfish ends and worldly comforts, but it will not lead to God realization. Any such practice with full and unshakable faith in God will lead to God realization. The essence of the folk festivals in Kosal region is Godrealization. People irrespective of caste, creed and religion gather in large number to witness the folk festivals and merge themselves whole heartedly with the spiritual action and reactions of the Barua. They witness the union of the Barua's soul (atma) with the super soul (Paramatma). Lakhs of people witness the spiritual drama with an utter sense of devotion. They worship the Barua as a deity and realize God in him or her during these folk festivals. This is the metaphysical discovery in such folk festivals by the author, where the varuas teach the mankind that such realization is possible through 'Samadhi'. Such a grand spiritual live drama is anacted in practical form which provides the basic spiritual life force to humanity. Thanks to our forefathers of Kosal region who have established such grand spiritual tradition by way of fok festivals hither to unknown to people of other parts of the world.

Printed by Libri Plureos GmbH in Hamburg,
Germany